This book was very loved
But we needed room for ne
We hope you will enjoy it
Just as much as we did, too.

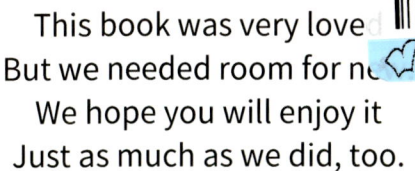

DATE DUE

NOV 2 3 1984		
NOV 2 2 1993		

Man Comes to America

Books by Harold Coy

THE AMERICANS
THE MEXICANS
MAN COMES TO AMERICA

MAN COMES TO AMERICA

by Harold Coy

Illustrated by Leslie Morrill

Little, Brown and Company
BOSTON   TORONTO

COPYRIGHT © 1973 BY HAROLD COY

ALL RIGHTS RESERVED. NO PART OF THIS BOOK MAY BE REPRODUCED IN ANY FORM OR BY ANY ELECTRONIC OR MECHANICAL MEANS INCLUDING INFORMATION STORAGE AND RETRIEVAL SYSTEMS WITHOUT PERMISSION IN WRITING FROM THE PUBLISHER, EXCEPT BY A REVIEWER WHO MAY QUOTE BRIEF PASSAGES IN A REVIEW.

FIRST EDITION

T 06/73

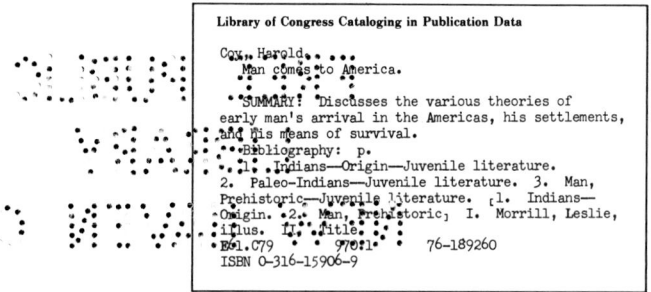

Library of Congress Cataloging in Publication Data

Coy, Harold.
    Man comes to America.

    SUMMARY: Discusses the various theories of early man's arrival in the Americas, his settlements, and his means of survival.
    Bibliography: p.
    1. Indians—Origin—Juvenile literature.
    2. Paleo-Indians—Juvenile literature. 3. Man, Prehistoric—Juvenile literature. [1. Indians—Origin. 2. Man, Prehistoric] I. Morrill, Leslie, illus. II. Title.
E61.C79   970'.1   76-189260
ISBN 0-316-15906-9

Published simultaneously in Canada by Little, Brown & Company (Canada) Limited

PRINTED IN THE UNITED STATES OF AMERICA

To the Indians
who discovered America

Contents

	Preface	ix
1	Like No Other Animal	1
2	Coming to Terms with the Cold	17
3	Who Came and When?	35
4	The Heyday of Hunting	55
5	Forest and Shore	73
6	Eskimo Lifeways	91
7	The Desert People	109
8	The Great Breakthrough	121
	Further Reading	139

Preface

THIS IS AN INDIAN STORY, though today's Indians, grazing sheep, working on high steel, or striving for a redress of old grievances, do not figure in it, nor do yesterday's Indians, paddling to a trading post with bundles of fur or making Custer die for our sins. Even Pocahontas, saving John Smith, and Squanto, teaching the Pilgrim Fathers to grow corn, go back no further, relatively speaking, than the day before yesterday.

This story is about Indians who discovered America and opened a hemisphere to mankind. It could not have been written very many years ago. Only as archaeologists recover early man's handiwork at hundreds of sites, estimating its age by radiocarbon dating and other methods, and studying it in collaboration with fellow scientists, is the story of man's coming to America unfolding.

Until recently, a New World date earlier than 1492 hardly existed except in Spanish-speaking America. where Aztec, Maya, and Inca traditions increased the time depth a century or two. Now, suddenly, we have discovered hunters spearing mammoths in Arizona in 9310 B.C., women weaving sandals in Oregon in 8100 B.C., polished stone axes and tiny cobs of domesticated corn, both 7000 years old, and a populous city in the Valley of Mexico contemporary with ancient Rome. Granted that the earliest dates may err by a few centuries, they nevertheless give us an exciting American past of respectable age. The Indians who reached America while the world was still in the grip of the Ice Age and pioneered in a new land are taking their proper and dignified place in the epic of mankind's dispersal over the face of the earth.

America at last has a prehistory that is several times as long as history that comes from written records. This book is a brief and simple report on its early highlights as scholars see them today. Scholars do not always agree among themselves. Science advances by means of hypotheses, that is, by conjectures that seem to fit the known facts. These hypotheses are subject to criticism and testing and are accepted, amended, or rejected as more facts come to light. The aim here is to present a balanced account, calling attention to the more important questions under debate.

Archaeological judgments depend on technical considerations that can only be hinted at here, among them, stratigraphy, tool, weapon, and pottery types, identification of extinct animals, pollen analysis, and the study of human remains, burial practices, and settlement patterns. A list of readings is appended for those who wish to go deeper into a fascinating subject.

HAROLD COY

Mexico, D.F.

1
Like No Other Animal

A HUNDRED AND SOME THOUSAND YEARS AGO, hippopotamuses drowsed the warm day long in pools beside the rivers of Europe, their blunt noses lifted from the water. In the cool of the evening they waded out on short, agile legs and gorged on lotus leaves to sustain their four tons and more of bulk.

The climate was so warm that Mediterranean shellfish inhabited northern seas. Rhinoceroses and straight-tusked elephants crashed through the underbrush in Central Europe. On the plains stretching eastward from the Netherlands were great herds of shaggy bison and smaller wild horse herds, each led by a wise old stallion.

Cave hyenas of those times have left us samples of their daggerlike teeth and bone-crushing molars. There were lions where London is now, and no doubt they worked in relays as lions still do, some driving the prey and others lying in reserve, until finally one of the fiercest, a lioness, made the kill.

Predators abounded: the wolf pack, tireless in running down an elk; the brown bear with a sweet tooth for honey and a forepaw strong enough to strike down a deer; and the wolverine, poised on a branch to leap upon a larger animal and go for the jugular vein.

Among the rarer predators was man. He didn't seem cut out to be a hunter. In place of claws he had nails that hardly served to scratch his fleas. He lacked a snout with which to seize his food, and his teeth were pitiful weapons even for defense. He was unable to twist his ears so as to pick up small cues of sound, and he couldn't smell at all compared to the big cats. Small martens leaped from branch to branch after squirrels, and fawns ran swiftly beside their mothers when pursued. Not man. Even when grown he was no match for the jackal in the chase. Running overheated him, and he had sweat glands instead of body hair. His skin was not thick like an elephant's nor covered with bristles like a boar's. That overgrown wild cow, the aurochs, had horns for goring and hoofs for kicking. But not man.

Nevertheless, man had a few things in his favor or he wouldn't have been present. He had good eyes. Standing on his hind limbs, he could look out over the tall grass and observe his prey in color and in three dimensions. His hands were free for manipulation. And he had become clever since his prehuman forebears had discovered that one can not only throw a stone but can break it and get a cutting edge. His brain was now three times as large as it had been then. It guided his hands in fashioning weapons that took the place of fangs and claws. It stored up memories and foresaw what was not yet but might be, like a potential knife in a lump of stone or a spear in a green yew stick.

Spear in hand and companions around him, man found courage to drive the fire-hardened spear tip between an elephant's ribs. Patiently he followed the great beast's trail of blood. Trustingly he joined with his fellows in the kill.

Elephant flesh though was not man's daily fare. He was more familiar with venison and horsemeat and, for that matter, with hare and mouse. His woman and children caught slow game like tortoises and frogs. They robbed birds' nests, dug roots, and gathered mushrooms. Man and his family were omnivorous, like the rat and the pig. They ate almost everything, and though they couldn't eat grass, pine bark, or linden leaves, they ate the animals that did.

Man's very physical weakness was an asset insofar as it had forced him to learn to cooperate. He'd come a long way, 100,000 years ago, since that much remoter time when his ancestors, in response perhaps to changing climate, had left the trees, with their luscious fruit and buds, to forage on the African plains. Compare man with his distant cousin, the chimpanzee. Though the latter belongs to a troop for mutual defense, each chimp finds its own food, even mothers with infants. Man had to become, in some respects, less like an ape and more like a wolf. The wolf, for all his bad name, is a loyal member of the pack and an excellent provider, bringing meat to the den for his mate and pups. Man's line became human only after forming similar attachments in the course of hundreds of thousands, even millions of years.

We can picture our earliest plains-dwelling ancestors searching in small bands for the sparse provender the savanna offered, if not vegetable food, then animal. They were perforce meat-eaters, catching reptiles and rodents and possibly disputing with jackals and vultures the carrion that lions had left uneaten. These puny, not yet human creatures, still a bit unsteady on their hind legs, scarcely deserve the name of hunters until the time when they could attack with sticks and stones and knock a few flakes from a river pebble to give it a cutting edge.

Hunters with the imagination to do these things killed larger animals, ate better, lived longer, and left more and brighter descendants. A good brain had what biologists call survival value. And so over the millennia

the brain of man in the making became not only better, but so wonderfully complex that, unlike a baby chimp's brain, it needed more than twelve months to reach its full development. It required many years to grow, starting from helpless infancy — and this awkward necessity was to have tremendous consequences for the human race. A mother whose children were slowly maturing in mind and body could not be out

for days stalking antelope. She had to stay near a home base, though it was only a temporary campsite behind a windbreak. Her man, returning there from the chase, found a welcome, provided he brought home the bacon, so to speak. Before he knew it, he was as good as married, and to just one wife. And one was enough: only his remote descendants would hunt well enough to covet two or three.

There was much to be said for monogamy, though man was perhaps still unable to say it in words. He did not have to fret away a lonely youth while some fractious old baboon jealously guarded a numerous harem. Unlike a stag, he didn't butt heads with a rival in the mating season, or lock antlers in a fatal embrace. Nor did he risk becoming a loner in old age, like a peevish bull elephant, for after his children were grown there were grandchildren to admire how cleverly he chipped stone, and kinsfolk of various degrees with whom he feasted from time to time.

The one-wife rule made man more trusting of other men and readier to join them in the hunt. Alone he might spend all day throwing stones without hitting a rabbit, but a hunting team beating the bushes could drive a hundred of the prey into an enclosure. Larger animals too were vulnerable if several men joined to attack and pursue them. And two heads, or twelve, were better than one in devising a new way of taking game, like a pitfall concealed by leafy branches or a pair of throwing stones tied together with a thong in such a way as to entangle the legs of a running animal.

Equally important were tools for chopping through hide and sinew and straight-edged scrapers for dressing skins. Benjamin Franklin said, "Man is a toolmaking animal," which is true, though a chimpanzee also makes a tool when he strips off a sapling and pokes it into a termite nest. Man, however, makes more elaborate tools, and not always for immediate use. He learns the art from his fellows and teaches it to his children. Each tool comes to be made according to a set pattern. Once man's way of life depended on standardized tools, so much so that he could not do without them, he may be said to have crossed the threshold of humanity.

In this sense we became human as much as a million years ago, though some scientists, using other definitions, say it was even earlier. Then, during hundreds of thousands of years, we spread through Africa, into southern Europe and Asia, and up the seacoasts as far as England and northern China. For man, a tropical animal, to adapt himself to temperate climates and cold winters without so much as growing a woolly coat was an achievement largely due to his expanding brain. Growing in self-awareness, bound to his family and kinsmen by ties of affection and interest, he met each new challenge by learning and teaching. What man does from having been taught is known as culture. It is different from the instincts that move beavers to

build dams and birds to make nests. Built-in behavior patterns like these are acquired only in the course of countless generations. Culture is infinitely quicker. If it occurs to a hunter to disguise himself with a set of antlers and creep up on a deer, he can pass on the trick to his son, just as a mother can train her daughter to watch the hearth fire and keep it smoldering.

Long before man learned to make fire, he must have captured it from some lightning-kindled conflagration. Otherwise he could hardly have endured the cold of his new habitats. And it would have been dangerous to sleep in a cave without a fire burning at its mouth, for man shares with apes the habit of snoring, and if the leopards had not smelled him they would surely have heard him. Fire also supplied light to work by and heat for cooking. It hardened the tips of wooden spears.

Fire was itself sometimes a hunting weapon. Some 300,000 years ago, an elephant herd was diverted into a Spanish bog, there to flounder and die under the spears and stones of man. Traces of ash found at the site suggest that the hunters had set the dry grass afire to deny the heavy-footed animals escape and drive them to their doom. Among the stone tools left lying about were the hand axes man supposedly used to pierce the elephants' hides and dig into their skulls for brains and the cleavers with which he hacked the joints and smashed the huge bones for marrow.

A gory scene. Remember, though, that man was always a hunter until a few thousand years ago, or say during ninety-nine percent of his possible million years as a human being. Generation after generation, forty thousand times over perhaps, father taught son to stalk game and find pleasure in killing. This was something foreign to man's vegetarian relatives like the gorilla, who, despite a belief to the contrary, is relatively gentle. The impetus of this long tradition is with us yet. Man's readiness at times to go beyond the tiger and the wolf and kill his own kind remains a problem to this day, graver now than ever. However, what is taught can be untaught.

At the same time, it was only by hunting that man became human. An ape dining on the succulent shoots of a tree, which doesn't fight back or run away, feels no urge to make weapons. To do one thing for very long bores the ape: his attention span is brief. By contrast, man, pitting himself against animals, some of them large and fierce, acquired toolmaking skills, habits of close observation, and patience in tracking. He studied animal behavior and knew the game trails, the water holes, and the seasons. He enjoyed the affection of his family and the trust of his hunting partners. Sharing the game with them and with the old and sick, he became aware of rights and obligations. He learned to control his temper and act more with his head and less with his glands. He developed a sense of right and wrong and a human conscience.

Somewhere along the line man went beyond gestures and cries to express what was on his mind but not before his eyes. He began talking; no one is sure exactly when. It's been said that man's erect posture left not only his hands free for grasping but his mouth for chattering, and that he had to have language to explain to his pupils how tools were made. And how, it is asked, could man communicate with his hunting companions without using words? One answer might be that dogs and lions do very well without speech. Yet good as they are for hunting together, these animals are marked off in one way from even the simplest human hunting band. Dogs have no uncles that they know of, and no lion acknowledges a brother-in-law. They mate without regard for kinship. But human beings, presumably from the earliest times, have avoided marriage with close relatives. This has served to head off jealousies within the household and to encourage marriage alliances with neighboring bands. It has prevented close inbreeding and widened the pool from which future generations were to draw their inheritance. At some point, certainly, man found language indispensable for maintaining his social contacts and passing on his expanding culture.

Man's culture expanded rather slowly for half a million years or more, after that first bold surge into Asia and Europe. Africa remained a motherland from which new tools spread to the northern edges of the human world. The widely used hand ax was one of these, a pointed tool, made by chipping flakes from the surface of a water-worn pebble. It served to lop off a branch, stab a rhino, skin a gnu, or grub up an edible root. A straighter, sharper cutting edge was achieved when man learned to remove wide, shallow flakes not with a stone hammer but with a softer one of wood or bone. These waste flakes were useful for planing wood and slicing meat. Eventually the flint chippers began making flake tools on purpose. They would shape what they wanted on a core of stone, then dislodge it with a single deft blow, ready for use after perhaps a little retouching around the edges. More than once improvements like these spread over western Europe, but then there were long stretches of time when glacial ice crept down from the mountains and the hand-ax people pulled back toward Africa, like the game they hunted.

What was happening in eastern Asia at this time is less understood but no less important for our story. Toolmaking there took a different path. Instead of trimmed-down hand axes, we find craggier implements made from pebbles, lumps of rock, and thick flakes. They look bulky and shapeless but have been chipped to provide a working edge, especially for scraping and chopping.

Over the ages the brain that guided the hands that made these various tools kept bulging out and folding in on itself to make room for all the incoming messages, switching stations, motor controls, and memory storage areas that, so to speak, enter into the working of the human mind. All this took time and possibly accounts for man's slow development. Human fossils are too rare for very firm dates, but many scientists now suspect that man may have qualified as a member of our own species, *Homo sapiens*, 200,000 or more years ago. That is earlier than anyone imagined back in the days when only a man who looked much like ourselves was accepted as *sapiens*, meaning wise.

Thus we return without too big a jump to the warm times of 100,000 years ago, give or take 20,000 years or so. We see man as short of stature and low of crown. We do not know how he was dressed, if at all, though a rabbit-skin cape would have been comfortable at night even in a mild climate. Life was hard and brief. Skeletal remains show that men seldom lived past forty or women past thirty. Both suffered from parasites, arthritis, sinus infections, and bad teeth. The bones they smashed and tossed aside reveal their special fondness for marrow and brains. Occasionally they treated human bones in suspicious ways, but whether man ate his neighbor — if he did — from hunger or with the pious intent of absorbing his good qualities we can only guess.

Whatever man's frailties of body and spirit, something new was now stirring inside him. After the slow pace of half a million years, man was developing many new kinds of tools, both in the West and as far away as China's Yellow River. He was moving onto the northern German plain, and there, at Ehringsdorf, the earliest known stone projectile points have been found. Thinned down on both sides and presumably mounted on shafts, they could be thrown or thrust into the flanks of big game with a deadlier impact than wooden spears.

Man didn't yet make beads or paint pictures, so far as we know, but he had become a fine craftsman whose hand axes reveal lines more graceful than those required for pure utility. He was an artist, almost, possessing foresight and sensibilities like no other animal's. Anthropologists have a saying, "An animal knows, but only man knows that he knows." Yet man, if we may judge from simple hunting peoples of later times, did not know he was different in this respect. He imagined that his fellow creatures, and even the trees and the wind, had feelings and thoughts like his own and the power to do him good or harm.

In fact, man seems to have attributed superhuman powers to some animals, especially the shaggy cave bear, who towered eight feet when reared on his hind legs in anger. These huge beasts roamed the Alpine woodlands and went to hibernate in caves in such numbers that after many winters they rubbed the walls smooth. Awake or napping, they were a challenge to

man's new powers. There was less perilous game on the plains, but some urge to excel drew man up eight thousand feet into the Alps to the lair of his most formidable adversary. The cave bear could take punishment from man's weapons and still fight on. This we know from the fact that some bear bones show mended fractures. Impudent little man, a monkey's cousin with a spear, must often have paid with his life for the temerity of going into the cold mountains, looking for trouble.

Perhaps man was struggling with his own fears as much as with the bear. He was afraid not only of the bear's crushing paw but of what the bear, even when dead, might do in retaliation. At least we may imagine this from the concern later hunters have shown for the injured feelings of animals, which seemed to them so human but which they nevertheless butchered and ate.

Alpine hunters not only slew the bears but took over their cave retreats. Afterward they paid reverence to a worthy foe by displaying the bears' skulls in niches in the cave walls. To us this suggests the pride of hunting trophies, but man of those times probably was stirred by deeper feelings of awe or guilt. In one Swiss cave he put his bear skulls away in a stone chest and set the long bones neatly along the walls. Was this magic to bring luck in the hunt? Was it an act of atonement, an offering laid on an altar to some powerful bear spirit? Was it a sacrifice, perhaps, of something precious, since neither the tasty brains nor the marrow had been consumed? Who knows? We should not read the thoughts of later hunters into the minds of men so long dead, except to say that man already had come to feel for the cave bear something that no other animal feels for its prey.

2
Coming to Terms with the Cold

Some 70,000 years ago or more the climate turned cold — and so it remained, fluctuating up and down but always chilly, until within 10,000 years of our time. This long freeze came on too gradually to be noticed in one lifetime. Yet over the millennia it sculptured a new landscape, uprooted plants and animals, and reshaped man's destiny.

Why this upheaval occurred — and others like it in the remoter past — is a not fully solved mystery, involving solar radiation, ocean currents, land forms, and the prevailing winds. The first signs appeared, as before, in the mountains, where more snow began falling in the winter than the summer sun could melt. The new snow, bearing down on the layers beneath, compacted them into ice. As the pressure increased, the ice became plastic and began to flow. Icy tongues crept down the valleys. They merged into frozen masses that tumbled from cliff faces and fell into the sea as icebergs or spread in sheets over the plains, mowing down forests and grinding rock to powder.

Whenever the summer temperature rose above the freezing point, the ice edges melted. Wind-blown rock dust then laid a mantle of fine loam over the frozen subsoil bordering the glaciers. Eventually the new soil, moistened by meltwater, gave sustenance to cold-resistant grasses and shrubbery. Lichens spread over the rocks. The warmest days brought forth wildflowers like those that blossom today in pastures above the tree line. Country like this is called tundra and has few trees except perhaps aspen and dwarf willow. Much of Central Europe, for example, was tundra in the coldest times. Farther south grew birch or spruce and pine, retreating or advancing with the swings of the climate.

Animals, no less than trees, underwent changes. Some perished or took refuge in the South. The ibex and the chamois, already inured to cold, descended from the mountains. Out of the Far North came reindeer, thousands together, their many-forked antlers bending and tossing. Woolly mammoths, with a thick

fur insulation piled on their warm undercoats, grew fat on tundra grass. The two-horned woolly rhinoceros, a browser, moved with the seasons, leaving the brushy plains to winter at the forest edge. Each animal, if it survived, adapted to a cold world after its fashion.

Man also had to come to terms with the dreadful cold. During earlier glacial advances, he'd retreated like any other animal or at most had taken a stand no farther north that we know of than Hungary and Peking. But this latest glaciation found him better prepared for the challenge. He endured the ice and learned to survive in a truly arctic climate. He even pushed north into still colder country.

The first of these hardy pioneers were the Neanderthals. Now Neanderthal Man is often thought of inaccurately. He is the cave man of the comic strips, a barrel-chested fellow with a face sitting forward on a low skull that bulges at the sides and behind. And what a big, ugly face! Sloping forehead, beetle brows, sunken eyes, high nose, big teeth, no chin at all. You see him clubbing his rivals and dragging his woman by the hair. Fortunately the picture is exaggerated. Neanderthal Man, though not entirely cleared of cannibalism, was doubtless as peace-loving as we are today, if only because he hadn't much to fight about and needed companions for the arduous food quest. As for his looks, not all Neanderthal skeletons show characteristics as pronounced as do the ones originally found in the caves of western Europe, where inbreeding had been going on for thousands of years in what must have been a glacier-bound, out-of-the-way corner of the world.

Handsome or not, Neanderthal Man was progressive for his times. His brain was if anything slightly larger than ours, though whether it was as complex we don't know. At any rate he was smart enough to keep from freezing and starving in the bleakest surroundings man had ever lived in. He wore clothing of some kind on the hunting trail, to judge by all the flint scrapers he made, presumably for dressing hides. He learned how to shape a lump of stone so that one flake after another could be broken off, ready to serve as blanks for new and more efficient tools.

Neanderthal Woman gathered berries and nuts during the short growing season, but human survival depended on a good supply of meat. There were bands in southern France that maintained a year-round hunting base at the mouth of a cave. And there were other hunters who wintered in the forest and moved with the spring thaw through quagmires and clouds of biting flies to the edge of the tundra. At Lebenstedt in north central Germany a summer camp of some 55,000 years ago has been uncovered. The heaps of bone there obviously were left by highly specialized hunters, since three-fourths of the slain animals were reindeer. Mammoths account for another seventh of the total, and from their ribs were made the oldest known bone spear points.

Magic was just as important as weapons. Deep in an Italian cave are the footprints of Neanderthal hunters who milled about lobbing clay pellets at a stalagmite that resembled an animal in shape. No doubt they believed that if they hit the mark they would do the same on the trail. At certain other sites, Neanderthal Man scratched animal designs on bone, not so much for art's sake, probably, as for meat's sake. Yet he was artist enough to use pigments and crayons, presumably to paint his body. In northern Iraq, an old man of forty — and forty *was* old 50,000 years ago — was buried with an offering of wildflowers, or so the pollen mixed in with the grave soil leads us to believe. Remembered in death, he had been looked after with kindness in life, for he was a cripple with a withered right arm, unable to hunt as other men did.

Fifty thousand years ago or thereabouts a chapter opens in human history that has been called the second expansion of mankind. Not since man spread out from the African plains several hundred thousand years before had there been such a movement into new lands.

Below the Sahara, an inhospitable rain forest was encroaching on the savanna. Here in due course man learned to make wooden implements and thrusting weapons and to take game at short range in the jungle.

On a colder front, man occupied the river valleys of Russia. Finding no caves, he built his own shelters. By the Dniester River are the walls of an ancient house, consisting of a ring of mammoth tusks and bones.

From the Middle East man crossed the mountains to the shores of the Black Sea and spread over the Central Asian deserts as far as Mongolia. Some years ago a boy's grave was uncovered in Uzbekistan. Around it were six pairs of Siberian mountain goat horns, placed there perhaps to watch over his spirit. The child, though Neanderthal-like in some traits, had a domed skull not unlike that of modern man, meaning ourselves.

His is not the only hint of the shape of heads to come. Others appear in North Africa and in southern Asia and the Near East. About 40,000 years ago the hints, coming from various parts of the world, are firm and sure. Fully modern man, with a smooth brow and a well-rounded head, is waiting to make his entrance on the scene. In Europe, where he is best known, he appears during a break in the cold spell around 37,000 years ago, but this is probably not his premiere. He multiplies and within a thousand years or so becomes the prevailing type of human kind.

This is a sudden appearance as human evolution goes. It raises questions. Did modern man spread out from a homeland, like the Middle East, or was he emerging simultaneously in many places? Did he evolve out of Neanderthal Man or were they cousins with a common ancestor? How often, in their wanderings, did the two lines meet and mate? Though these questions are far from answered, scientists have come to recognize that the two branches of men are fairly close kin. They tend now to classify them as subdivi-

sions of the same species, namely *Homo sapiens neanderthalensis* and *Homo sapiens sapiens*. By this reckoning, we of all presently living races are twice *sapiens*, or doubly wise men.

Modern man continued the peopling of the earth that Neanderthal Man had begun. His trail is marked by long, narrow tools made from flint blades. He removed the blades from a stone core by striking a hammerstone against a wood, bone, or antler punch. His improved technique gave him several times as much cutting edge from a lump of flint as Neanderthal Man had obtained.

Blade tools are best known from digs in France, but they were made as far away as the Chinese-Mongolian borderlands where the Great Wall now stands. Yet there seems to be no close connection between the two areas. In the East, moreover, the old persists beside the new. Along with knives and points of advanced design there are flake tools resembling those of Neanderthal times and even a few choppers of a yet older vintage, which were still being made in Southeast Asia.

This odd mix is mentioned for its bearing on later contacts with eastern Siberia, which is not known to have been inhabited at this time. It was a cold land, colder sometimes at high latitudes in the interior than the North Pole. Yet somehow man reached the long arm of Siberia that extends into the Far Northeast. It has been common to imagine him following cold-weather animals there, over the great plain that stretches four thousand miles eastward from Central Europe. Europe has been so well explored that there are some clues by which to trace a plausible route. But perhaps this was only one of the migratory currents, and not the earliest, that passed into eastern Siberia. China, Mongolia, and Central Asia were all closer than Europe, and hunters from any or all of these lands could have been moving northward. In recent years, Chinese, Japanese, and Russian archaeologists have been digging for weapons and tools in order to throw light on ancient travel patterns, which, we may be sure, will turn out to be more complicated than the flow of expressway traffic.

Whatever man's routes, he must have shivered, for a new ice advance began 26,000 years ago. On and on came the glaciers until some thirty percent of the earth's surface was covered, a mile deep in some places. Not for hundreds of thousands of years had it been so cold — and the climate didn't get much warmer until 12,000 years ago.

In fearfully cold eastern Siberia there was little glaciation, strange to say, except in the mountains. On the frozen plains the air, though it cut like a knife, was too dry and the rainfall and snowfall were too slight for glaciers to form. The tundra was open to people able to endure the exceptional rigors of the climate. And it offered them magnificent hunting.

Candidates for life on this most frigid of tundras must have passed through what one anthropologist has called a "cold filter." All but the hardiest were screened out. Those most likely to succeed were already adapted in some measure to the cold. There come to mind the descendants or successors of the specialized hunters of northern Germany and of the men who built huts of mammoth bone in Russia. But we should not overlook northern China, where, even before *Homo sapiens* came into being, Peking Man was sucking marrow from deer bones in his commodious cave at Choukoutien. People had been living there ever since, acclimated to cold winds from the Mongolian plains and ready perhaps to face severer weather still.

To illustrate how man could survive and prosper under conditions of extreme cold, we turn to the examples at hand. The best of these happen to be one in Central Europe and one in the heart of Siberia, though neither place was necessarily a stopover at that time on the way to the Far Northeast.

It was more than 20,000 years ago that a band of related families established a year-round hunting station at Dolni Vestonice in Czechoslovakia. The site overlooked a mammoth trail, so the hunters killed the big elephants in great numbers and stacked the bones in neat piles, ready to serve as building materials or as fuel for their hearths. The dripping fat made a welcome blaze in a cold land poor in timber.

Since wood was scarce, especially hardwood, piercing implements were chipped from flint or, better, carved from strips of flexible bone. An ordinary flint knife wouldn't cut grooves in bone. It took a burin, a tool with a chisellike cutting edge backed up by a full thickness of stone — and burins were made in abundance. There were also bone whistles and flutes, which would have been useful for decoying animals. This is not to say that the people of Dolni Vestonice were insensitive to music and art. They worked antler and mammoth ivory into objects of use and beauty and wore necklaces strung with animal teeth of local origin and seashells from far away. Neanderthal Man and his wife had never adorned themselves with so much finery!

That these people had definite religious ideas is evidenced by the rhino, ibex, and mammoth heads they made of baked clay, presumably to gain power over the coveted game animals. More impressive still is a female figurine, modeled in the prevailing taste with ample hips and bosom. She is one of many found from France to Siberia and known as Venus figures. What do they signify? According to one theory, they reflect the enhanced prestige that woman came to enjoy after hunting groups set up more or less permanent camps. For then she ceased being a mere bearer of burdens for a wandering band and became the keeper of hearth and home, the one who took thought for the morrow. Besides preparing skins for clothing, she put meat away in the natural deep-freeze of an underground pit and rationed it out in the lean times between the semiannual game migrations. So indispensable was woman, it is speculated, that the Venus figure came to symbolize a great mother from whom the hunting band reckoned their common descent. And, having power to transmit life from generation to generation, she was conceivably akin to the "mistress of the game" to whom later peoples looked to replenish the supply of animals.

Man's constant preoccupation with game is recorded in France and Spain on cavern walls, where artists painted the wild ponies, humped bison, forked reindeer, and tall bulls and cows so devoutly wished for. They used charcoal and mineral pigments with a fine feeling for shading, color, and line and showed the animals falling under the spell of sorcerers or being pierced by spears and spurting blood. Inside a cave in Russia's Ural Mountains is a frieze displaying bear, deer, horses, and mammoths, while some of the paintings on Siberian cliffs are said to date from the great freeze.

Animals, grass-eating and flesh-eating, had preceded man on the rolling grasslands of Siberia and the marshes that gave firm footing when frozen. They had worn paths over the low divides and down to the lightly wooded streams. They had come to terms with the cold. Musk-oxen, acclimated to the cruel winters, huddled together in their drooping fur, breathing out clouds of vapor. Reindeer broke the crusted snow with their hoofs and fed on reindeer moss. The Arctic fox burrowed into a snowdrift and muffled his face with his tail, while the ptarmigan's very feet were feathered.

Man too confronted the awful cold — and without fur, feathers, or a bushy tail. The sweat from his feet or the vapor from his breath could freeze him stiff if he went unprotected. An ivory figure carved in those days portrays him in fur garments with fitted sleeves. Samples of his belt fasteners and bone needles have come down to us. He surely wore mittens and footgear. To shelter himself from the arctic wind, he built his skin-covered hut half underground and crawled into it by a tunneled passageway.

People of diverse traditions seem to have met and mingled on the steppe and tundra around Lake Baikal in east central Siberia. Malta, the region's best-known site, dates from an estimated 15,000 to 20,000 years ago. Choppers and scrapers found there are like those in the Chinese-Mongolian borderlands, though they could have come from Central Asia. There are stone spear points, thinned on both faces and shaped like laurel leaves, that would inflict a penetrating wound and tire the largest animal from loss of blood. Are they derived from earlier ones made in this style in western Siberia and Russia? There are three expert opinions on this: yes, maybe, and no. Uncertainty also surrounds the richer aspects of Malta's culture, like the splendid bone and ivory carving. It has been considered of European inspiration, though of late Asian influences are also suspected.

It is possible to reconstruct in imagination something of domestic life in Malta. The earthen house walls were reinforced with stone slabs, antlers, rhino horns, and mammoth tusks as much as two yards long. The roofing was a framework of poles covered with hides. Men and women warmed themselves at separate hearths. On the left was the women's side. It is identified by the bone needles and hairpins found there, along with "mother figures" carved in mammoth ivory with elegant hairdos. The men's side was for hunting implements and, in one house at least, for carvings of waterfowl, such as a swan in flight. Were these birds magical representations of game to be snared? Or did they mark an early stage of the shaman cult which continued in this region into our own times? A shaman was a supersorcerer. He would fall into a trance, uttering bird calls, while his spirit was believed to soar birdlike into the skies and plead with the awesome powers who ruled there to send the people health and plenty of game.

A four-year-old child's burial allows us a glimpse of the religious practices. An ivory band rested upon the forehead, and ivory bracelets and beads encircled the wrists and throat. The body had been sprinkled with red ocher, the color of blood and life, and had been laid facing the east, where the sun is reborn.

Little is known of man's presence in this region before Malta. Perhaps earlier hunters had set their faces to the rising sun and by veering north had penetrated to the remotest reaches of Siberia and beyond. If so, they surely traveled light and would hardly have carried jewels and figurines to this bleak frontier, even if they had possessed them. If they came as early as some authorities believe, they would have lacked a knowledge of hafted tools, barbed fish spears, and spear-throwing sticks that worked the near-magic of doubling the propelling power of a hunter's arm. These inventions came trailing after, in the hands of later migrants or in the hunting lore that was passed on from one band to another.

Perhaps the very first men to reach northeastern Siberia were simple hunters and fishermen unequipped for specializing in big game. If they came before the heartland of Siberia was peopled, they are likely to have arrived from the south, from beyond the Mongolian deserts, perhaps, or from down the coast in the direction of China. A route not too far from the Pacific would have brought the moderating influences of the warm sea currents. Travelers might even have followed the shoreline of northern Japan, which in the coldest times was attached to Siberia. That is because during the Ice Age, and particularly in its severest phases, a great deal of the world's water was withheld from the seas and locked up in glaciers. Ocean levels dropped, and land now submerged rose from the deep.

At the Bering Strait a land bridge several hundred miles wide then joined Siberia with Alaska. Over it, living creatures could pass into a New World. So similar are the animals on both sides of this onetime bridge that many of them clearly did so.

Foxes and wolves, as well as certain species of bison, deer, bear, and elephants, had crossed during earlier glaciations, before man, so far as we know, was capable of surviving in the Far North. The bridge, incidentally, carried two-way traffic. Such New World natives as ancestral camels and horses passed over it to Asia, where they might have met woolly rhinos that had come the other way but were now languishing on tundras bare of brush and were never to make it to the bridge. The cowlike yak tried a little harder and reached Alaska but died out there, most unfortunately, for in the fulness of time it might have been a useful beast of burden.

The woolly mammoth was a latecomer, like the reindeer, which after some small changes became the caribou. The bridge was there to receive them around 40,000 years ago and, if they missed it then, was open again during the long, cold period that started about 26,000 years ago.

While these desirable game animals were changing worlds, was man present to observe them? If so, he would surely have followed them. He might have speared the stragglers and weaklings of the larger species, or, failing that, existed on Arctic hares, smaller rodents, and fish. Early or late, he set eyes on the game and then, trapping and tracking, he came, all unknowing, to America. The question is: When?

3
Who Came and When?

EARLY IN THE PRESENT CENTURY it was generally believed that man had been in America no more than a few thousand years. Then in 1926, near Folsom, New Mexico, the bones of some long-extinct bison were found exposed in a ravine that had cut its way down to Ice Age levels. Buried in the rib cage of one animal was a spear point, clearly the work of a skillful hand. It was one of nineteen Folsom points, and they were convincing proof that man had been in America early enough to hunt the wide-horned bison.

Since that discovery, techniques have been developed for measuring the radioactive carbon still present in once living tissue and thereby estimating its age. By this means, other sites with similar points have been judged to be 10,000 to 11,000 years old. Man's presence in America was pushed back at least a thousand years more with the discovery of still earlier points, including a type apparently meant for mammoth hunting. There the matter stood for many years. Man was allowed 12,000 years in the New World, plus a thousand or so more to get from Siberia to one or another of the big-game sites that were being discovered from Wyoming to Arizona. This much could be proved, but proposals for assigning American man a greater age were dismissed as speculative or resting on loose evidence.

There was reason for this caution. False alarms have been frequent in studies of early man. Various discoveries that seemed to put man in America a very long time ago did not stand up under independent criticism — or at least failed to convince. What to one archaeologist is a cache of primitive tools, to another may be a pile of stones knocked about by flowing water. Even radiocarbon dates are subject to error from contamination or faulty technique. What is tested also matters. Samples of charcoal from Lewisville, Texas, going back 40,000 years, are the oldest dated evidence of man in America if, as some believe, they really come from hearths where he roasted the flesh of glyptodons and camels. Others are skeptical. The supposed hearths, they say, may be only burnt woodrat nests.

Ironclad proof of early man's presence is not easy to come by. Ideally, his tools, if not his bones, should lie embedded in a layer of earth that ties in with some known geological event. The implements should be like those used elsewhere at the time. They should be accompanied by the remains of extinct animals. Animal or vegetable matter from the same stratum should be radiocarbon dated. If these clues jibe, you have a firm date.

Few discoveries meet all these requirements, and so any claim that man has been in America more than

13,000 or 14,000 years meets with resistance. Nevertheless, earlier dates continue to be reported, among them several from South America, and the feeling grows that not all of them can be wrong. A good many archaeologists, though by no means all, now accept at least the probability that man was in the New World much earlier than 13,000 years ago.

The question then remains: How much earlier? And it is linked to others. Did the early migrants arrive more or less at the same time or in several waves spaced far apart? Were they many or few? Did they come from a single region in Asia or from several? Were they of different stocks? What was their portal of entry to the New World? And what did they bring with them from the Old World?

In periods of extreme cold, when the land bridge was open, travelers could go dry-shod from Siberia to Alaska, as we have seen. They passed over a low rolling plain with tall grass and clumps of stunted trees. The climate may have been relatively mild for those frozen centuries, at least near the southern shore, for the bridge stood between the Arctic ice and the warmer Pacific. For generations of men the land mass was probably not so much a bridge as a homeland, which they left behind only when impelled by the food quest.

The bridge appeared and disappeared at various times during the long Ice Age. In its final phase, it offered a broad passageway to America, starting about 25,000 years ago and continuing, with interruptions toward the end, until the rising sea inundated it some 10,000 years ago.

For a long time, therefore, the way was open to Alaska and the top of North America. It was in reaching the heart of the continent that man must have met with difficulties, for the same freeze that let the land bridge emerge from the sea also set the ice in motion. Glaciers slid down Canada's western mountains to the sea and the plains. An ice sheet spread west from Labrador and Hudson Bay. The junction of these frozen masses laid a wall of ice across the breadth of Canada. From 23,000 to perhaps 10,000 years ago this barrier stood in man's way. It was impenetrable, according to some authorities, though others believe a corridor was open through it at times, especially after 13,000 years ago. But the middle range of this long period was so cold that the advancing ice blanketed the United States as far as the Missouri and Ohio rivers.

Here is a dilemma. When the land bridge was widest and most inviting, the ice barrier was rearing its formidable bulk. Was there an interval, perhaps, after the bridge had emerged but before the barrier was sealed, when Asian man could have reached the interior of North America? Some authorities believe that such a favorable time did exist between 25,000 and 23,000 years ago. After that, the temperature took such a dip that passage through the barrier may have been impossible for 10,000 years or longer. Man, however could, and likely did, move in behind it in Alaska and Canada. In the present stage of knowledge, we must allow for differences of a thousand years or so in these estimates. Nonetheless, they do illustrate the reasoning of those who hold that, if man came to America much earlier than 13,000 years ago, then he must have come well over 20,000 years ago.

If this is so, then once the ice barrier closed behind him, man must have been isolated from Old World influences for many thousands of years. It is argued that this is just what happened. Thus various toolmaking innovations — fine boneworking instruments like those of Dolni Vestonice and Siberian Malta, for example — did not spread beyond the barrier until the ice retreated. At the same time, the beautifully channeled and trimmed stone spear points that American hunters used toward the end of the Ice Age were too unlike anything known in the Old World to have come straight from there. Two theories have been proposed to explain them. One sees them as the culmination of a long series of New World refinements on early laurel-leaf points brought from Siberia. The other considers them a purely American invention, a replacement for older tips of bone, perhaps, or a slimming down of primitive stone tools too cumbersome to have served as hunting weapons.

The making of a thin stone point or knife is a far from simple art, yet it was practiced in Venezuela and Peru at least 10,000 years ago. Nearly 11,000 years ago, in a Patagonian cave, man was already making stemmed projectile points that apparently enabled him to feast on giant ground sloths. It is eleven thousand miles from the land bridge to this far tip of South America. So the sloth hunter's ancestors either made a fast trip or were already beyond the barrier when the big freeze came. Recently, even greater ages have been reported, among them 15,000 years for cuts on bone in Wilson Butte Cave in Idaho and 22,000 years for trimmed flake tools in central Mexico.

In 1971 an unusually interesting report was published, describing what was uncovered at various levels in a Peruvian highland cave near Ayacucho. Stone projectile points and skinning knives some 10,000 years old were found there, as elsewhere in South America. But deeper down were simpler, cruder points and implements, some made from bone. Mingled with them were remains of extinct animals, including a sloth bone 14,000 years old by radiocarbon dating. Still deeper lay choppers, scrapers, and wood-dressing tools roughed out from volcanic tuff. Here the dates ranged from 14,700 to 19,600 years ago, and the excavator believes that man may have come to this cave 22,000 years ago.

If man was in the Andes then, he was probably in North America much earlier. And that leads to the thorny question of whether there was a preprojectile-point stage, that is, a time when man was in America before he had learned to arm a shaft with a sharp stone point, or, for that matter, to put a handle on a tool. This much-disputed stage could take us back to migrations even earlier than the one we have imagined taking place 23,000 to 25,000 years ago. Its proponents do not shrink from the possibility that man may have come to America 40,000 or more years ago, during an earlier chapter in the history of the land bridge, bringing with him flake and chopper tools resembling yet older ones in Mongolia and China.

All this is a conjecture, to be confirmed or rejected as the truth that lies buried in the ground is uncovered. It attempts to account for assemblages of crudely worked stone tools and flakes that are found from time to time on old beaches and stream terraces in the western United States and on down through South America. Such tools are not easy to date. Sometimes they are on the surface of the ground, laid bare by the wind and keeping company with beer cans and discarded tire casings. They need not be of great age, since man kept on making crude choppers and scrapers for simple jobs long after he mastered newer techniques. Consequently, some archaeologists dismiss these finds as proving nothing. Others believe that a recent site should have some new tools mixed in with the old. But in many cases, all the stonework is rough and heavy, as if no one knew how to thin it down.

To sum up, we know that man was in America 13,000 years ago, and there are reasons accepted by many to believe he came 25,000 or perhaps even 40,000 years ago. Beyond that few experts will venture, though a controversial find of rough flakes in California's Mohave Desert has been estimated on geological grounds to be 50,000 to 80,000 years old. That would put man's first arrival back near the beginning of the last great glaciation.

If man reached America as much as 40,000 years ago, he came from an East Asia that was sparsely populated except in the general direction of China and points south. There man had deep roots, as we have seen, and there, in one of the caves at Choukoutien, among other places, he was still living late in the Ice Age. He was thoroughly modern now, so much so that a physical anthropologist has likened the skulls found at Choukoutien to those of "unmigrated American Indians." This was not to imply that the Indians came from precisely this spot, but rather that people resembling them were then living in this part of the world, ready to travel perhaps, but without any particular destination except to go where the food was.

If fortune led them on to discover America at a time when they lacked stone-tipped weapons, they would have relied on wooden spears and clubs, collective animal drives, and foraging for slow game. After them, we can imagine other, more numerous, hunters, coming from the Siberian tundra about 25,000 years ago, better equipped for taking big game but perhaps only a little better. Then there were the latecomers of 13,000 years ago and after. Many of them, discouraged by the advancing forests, no doubt preferred to stay on the northern tundra like the grazing and browsing creatures on which they preyed.

The great diversity of American Indian languages — some two thousand when the Europeans came — can be used to support either of two lines of argument: one, that innumerable migrant bands must have come from many Asian regions, speaking different tongues; or two, that if the original settlers spoke either a single language, or only a few, then thousands, even tens of thousands, of years are needed to account for the diversity of tongues. Only the Eskimos and Aleuts, late arrivals and not exactly Indians, share a common tongue with Asia. Linguistic scholars are sorting out the rest into a few great families, which may correspond to successive waves of migration into the New World. But so much time has gone by that even a distant relationship with the Old World is hard to discover — except possibly here and there along the North Pacific Coast.

Added to language diversity are all the differences in lifeways and physical traits. The Indians are at home in cold climates and hot, at sea level and high in the Andes. They are tall and short, stocky and slight of build, round- and long-headed, flat-nosed and hawk-nosed. The oldest skulls known in America — and there aren't many — tend to be long and narrow, with low foreheads and heavy brows. They have been called pre-Mongolian and may belong to a time before prominent cheekbones and flat faces were common in Asia. The Mongoloid face, with its eye fold and paddings of fat, may have evolved in the frozen north, it is theorized, for protection from the piercingly cold air. If the Mongoloid face is much attenuated among American Indians, that may be because they are descended from a mixture of peoples, some of whom came before the Mongoloid type was fixed.

Whatever their differences, Indians show a family resemblance in their brown eyes, black hair, usually straight, and scant body hair. The men have wispy beards, if any, and are seldom bald. Type-B blood is all but unknown among Indians, though it is common in Asia and not rare among Eskimos. This last fact is perhaps the strongest argument for the Indians' having come from a limited number of stocks, since otherwise they would have carried this blood type to America.

In any case, America was not peopled by tribes and nations on the march. A harsh terrain, at least at the outset, and the simple technology of the time would have kept the hunting units down to small bands and family foraging parties. It has been calculated that four hundred original settlers could have increased to ten million in the course of fifteen thousand years, especially with all the resources of an uncrowded New World open to them. Small groups, continually branching off and going their way, would have carried with them only part of the genes — the materials of inheritance — present in the parent band. In their descendants, certain traits would be accentuated, others eliminated. But how many millennia would go by before the noses in Valley X were noticeably bigger than in Valley Y no one at present is wise enough to say.

Whatever his Old World origins, man seems to have been already a modern man when he came to America. The oldest known skeletal remains mark him as belonging to the same species and subspecies that appeared in Europe some 37,000 years ago and may have existed elsewhere before then. If Neanderthal Man or his predecessors reached the New World, their remains have not been found. American man, as far back as we know him, was as much *Homo sapiens sapiens* as any of us — and more adventurous, perhaps, because he pushed out to farthest Asia and then two continents beyond.

The drama of man's coming to America stirs the imagination deeply and has led to unbridled speculation. Stories of lost tribes, far-ranging seafarers, and sunken continents whose survivors escaped to the New World have been told for generations and still may be heard. Similarities between the Indians and other peoples around the world have been singled out as evidence of American origins. Mankind being what it is, such likenesses are never hard to find but do not in themselves prove a connection.

Present-day scholars, having established man's presence in the New World in glacial times, see no way he could have come except via the Bering Strait region. Any other route would have called for seagoing craft such as were not built, it is believed, until after the Ice Age. Man may have reached Australia some 20,000 years ago, passing over short stretches of placid water in primitive floats, but the seaways to America were long and often stormy. Not even the Aleutian Islands, which seem on the map to link Asia with Alaska, are regarded as likely stepping stones for the earliest comers, considering the hazards of treacherous currents and poor visibility.

Skin boats probably were plying the waters around the Bering Strait soon after the land bridge disappeared, but thousands of years must have gone by before it was feasible to cross wide oceans. By then, distinctive Indian cultures already were in flower. A serious case has been argued for trans-Pacific crossings in comparatively late times, but any similar crossing of the Atlantic is at present only a matter of speculation.

What early man brought with him to America depends, of course, on when he came. At the very least he brought a knowledge of how to survive in the cold and how to hunt for his food. He surely could strike flint against iron pyrites, a mineral, and make a fire and undoubtedly he had some sort of shelter, if only consisting of a few skins laid over a framework of poles. And he must have warmed his body with skins, prepared no doubt by his wife's nimble fingers.

For the hunt, early man depended more on guile than weapons. He set snares and traps and used disguises to get within stabbing distance of his prey. If he came as early as some archaeologists believe, his first stone implements were primarily for butchering, skin dressing, and woodworking. In time he came to tip his spears with stone points, an art he learned by trial and error or that was brought by later arrivals from northern Asia. The latecomers may also have brought new techniques for fishing and hunting sea mammals. But much of the plant lore they may have had would have been lost on the bleak road to America, where there was so little to gather.

Early man no doubt twisted plant fibers into string but would not have bothered much with baskets until there were plant foods to carry. Three house plans, much alike in northern Asia and America, may have passed to the New World in relatively late times. These were the conical tipi, the oval or rectangular sweathouse, heated by steam or fire, and the half-underground dwelling with a tunneled entranceway. It would be comforting to imagine man's best friend accompanying him to the New World, but the dog appears only much later after being domesticated from the wolf in the Old World and perhaps also in the New. And it was only yesterday, archaeologically speaking, that the bow and arrow reached America after diffusing for thousands of years across Eurasia from its possible ancestral hearth in Africa.

As for the people, some passed on into North and South America, as we shall see, and some remained in the Northland and were the predecessors and perhaps in some part the ancestors of the Eskimos.

Man came to America not only with tools and weapons but with customs and beliefs, loyalties to family and band, hopes, fears, fancies, and songs. Two examples of his early art are known in Mexico: a piece of ancient camel bone carved in the likeness of a coyote's head, and some line drawings of yearned-for game — a tapir, a bison, an elephant — scratched on a wedge of mammoth bone. In Patagonia a rock painting is reported to represent masked dancers circling the guanacos they hoped to capture by their magic.

What else can we know of the thoughts of early Americans? Some of their ideas may have come down to us in tales told by Indians and collected by travelers and scholars. These, though recent in their present versions, often share a common theme with stories widely told in America, in northern Asia, and even throughout the world. This, of course, does not prove a common source. Imagination is found everywhere, and it may quite possibly occur to peoples at opposite ends of the earth that the sun is a great hunter pursuing the herds of stars. Each morning he slays them; each night they return to graze. But it is also possible that concepts like these were already in man's mind when he came to America. It is only a step from the story of the sun and the stars to the conviction that the animals a hunter kills do not permanently die, if he treats them with respect. Bear ceremonies, seemingly very old, persisted into modern times on both sides of the Bering Strait. The bear's head and paws, brightly adorned, were placed where all might see during a feast held in his honor. Though his own flesh was the main dish, such flattering speeches were made that his spirit departed and told the other bears not to be afraid of man.

Reverence for animal life may in fact be as old as

humanity. A hunter should take only so much game as was needed. Nothing should be wasted. And if he returned the blood to the earth and the bones to the water, then new animals would appear. This attitude lives on in our growing and quite rational concern that the earth's limited resources should not be needlessly squandered. To the ancients, wanton destruction was an affront to the great animal master, who could shut off the game supply at will. Then, as one story has it, a poor hunter might wander over the snowy wastes, lost, famished, crazed, and finally pursued by a cannibal spirit, half man and half animal.

In the New World as in the Old, the line between men and animals seemed vague and easily crossed. There were tales of animals living like people in secret places. Sometimes they wandered into our world in human form and took husbands or wives. They made good if touchy mates. A man with an otherwise perfect wife took care not to reproach her for a whiff of musky scent or she might turn herself back into a fox and run away, never returning.

Shamans, in Siberia and in America too, went about at night in animal guises. They called on animal helpers when, in trances, they flew to other worlds. They were the doctors of their time and much in demand, for a hunter too sick for the trail was in a sorry plight indeed. A shaman hunted like other men, and medicine was only his sideline, but it was amazing to watch him locate where his patient's trouble lay and suck it out in the form of a stick or a worm.

No magic could equal shaman magic except woman magic. A girl reaching puberty, the cycles marking her womanhood, and the birth of children were such incomprehensible signs of an awesome power that men around the world have felt the need for rites and tabus to safeguard their hunting luck from this stronger and stranger magic.

A bird perched on a limb might well be a baby waiting to be born. Birds had been present at the creation, according to a myth common to East Asia and America. Each bird dived in turn to the bottom of the all-encompassing waters, trying to bring up the mud that would form the earth. It was the loon that succeeded. Guiding the creation at the highest level was a force more easily felt than described. This Power or Being entrusted the smaller details to helpers, who unfortunately were less than perfect. Chief of these was the Trickster, who figures in the myths of every continent. In America he is Raven, Mink, Rabbit, or Coyote.

The Trickster is impulsive, thoughtless, and greedy. He can be crafty, as when he turns himself into a dish and steals the food placed on it. But often his tricks misfire and he plays the fool. He dives after berries he sees reflected in a stream and hits his head on a stone. He tries to capture a flock of swimming ducks by tying their legs together, but they take off in flight, carrying him with them. Believing himself as clever as the beaver, he dives under the ice for fish and can't get out. These cautionary tales were told to children to teach them good behavior.

On a generous impulse, the Trickster might do man a favor. He brought him light and fire and scattered salmon roe in the stream. But in his heedlessness he sowed misfortune too. He was so fond of ceremonies that he brought death into the world, considering it a lesser evil than doing without funeral services. One famous hoax of his is remembered in Siberia and America alike. The story goes that he pretended to be dead and then gobbled up the grave offerings. One of his projects was to make rivers on which man could float from place to place and rest his weary back. How the Trickster bungled that one, carelessly letting them all flow downstream! Man has been complaining ever since how much easier his lot would be if half the rivers ran upstream.

4
The Heyday of Hunting

WHENEVER MAN MAY HAVE COME to America, the fact is he arrived. And however he may have reached the heart of North America, we know that he did. His trail isn't easy to follow. When the Ice Age ended, the sea must have risen over campsites on the land bridge and the coastal shelf of Alaska. Other signs of man's passing lie congealed in the permafrost, the frozen subsoil of the tundra that archaeologists can explore only during the brief summer, and then, inch by painful inch, as it thaws. And these finds often prove to be of uncertain age or younger, even, than many sites farther south.

So we must take man where we find him and backtrack as best we can. A favorite starting point has been the Great Plains east of the Rockies. Here man's hunting and butchering tools have been found near the whitened bones of mammoths and bison. Here the fact that man was in America more than 10,000 years ago was first established.

The most obvious route to the Great Plains from the North was up the Mackenzie River Valley from the Canadian Arctic coast. And the way to the mouth of the Mackenzie was to continue from the land bridge across the top of Alaska. The northern foothills of Alaska's Brooks Range would have afforded man dry passage and a lookout for caribou grazing on the coastal plain. Weeks pass at this high latitude during which the winter sun never rises above the horizon. That man did nonetheless pass this way at one time or another is shown by a site on the Yukon Arctic coast, where stone tools of uncertain age have been found among bones of extinct bison.

So it's reasonable to speculate that man may have come to America by way of northern Alaska and the Mackenzie Valley. This does not necessarily mean that the first arrivals were equal to the heroic role once assigned them. An earlier and somewhat too simplified story line has man moving in relentless pursuit of big game all the way from Central Europe across Russia, Siberia, and Alaska, and finally up the Mackenzie and over Alberta to the tall grass of the Great Plains, from which he dispersed in his own good time to all parts of America. It's far from certain that any hunters were as proficient as that before they reached the New World and had a few thousand years in which to perfect their unique spear points. In any case, the right of the Plains hunters to be considered the first Americans is not as clear as once it seemed. Whoever did come first may well have made an unobtrusive entrance with simple weapons and a humble willingness to eat almost anything.

The possible great antiquity of some western finds

has led to a search for other doorways to America. For example, man could have gone from the land bridge over the flats of the winding Yukon River into the frigid interior of Alaska and the Canadian Yukon. Despite the cold, the lower valleys were glacier-free, and it was feasible to track game along the main river and its many tributaries. During warmer intervals, man could have crossed over mountain passes into other valleys, eventually reaching the Fraser River, the Plateau between the Coastal Ranges and the Rockies, and the Great Basin, which encompasses Nevada and parts of adjoining states. This was impossible, of course, in the middle period when ice blocked the high passes and blanketed British Columbia. But very early comers might have taken this way, just as latecomers apparently did 8,000 years ago when they spread beyond Alaska, carrying into the Plateau bone and ivory weapons studded with sharp bits of stone. There the new arrivals may have met their preglacial predecessors, some of them long since established on the Columbia River and others coming north from the Basin as the climate grew warmer.

Another route remains to consider. Could man have come down the Pacific coast from Alaska? Strong arguments are brought to bear against the feasibility of such a trip. How could early man, without boats or sleds, bypass the walls of glacial ice that came down to the sea? What would induce him to go hunting on sheets of ice bare of anything on which animals could feed?

Questions like these tend to eliminate the Pacific route. To a few scholars, however, it seems conceivable that during a warming interval the glaciers might have melted just enough on the seaward side to let man pass along the coastal shelf, living on seafood and such land animals as shared his route.

However it was that man put the ice behind him, he came eventually to paths already trodden by animals, and these he followed, over grasslands and along mountain flanks. Going up one river and over a divide to the headwaters of another, he blazed interregional trails. Bighorn sheep and Rocky Mountain goats must have stared from their crags as he passed between the Basin and the Plains. Unfortunately, we can only guess what his exact pathways may have been some tens of thousands of years ago. The rough, all-purpose tools attributed to him as of that time are too much alike, or perhaps too little studied yet, to be of much help in tracing routes. But they do indicate long-distance travel, being found all the way to southernmost South America.

As long as the riches of a new and uncrowded world lay open before him, even the simplest forager had security. If elephants were too big for him to bring down, prairie dogs, turtles, or tubers were never lacking. Elaborate weapons were unnecessary.

The earliest known spear points in the New World are made from bone splinters or from stone flakes chipped on one face. It is when the points are carefully

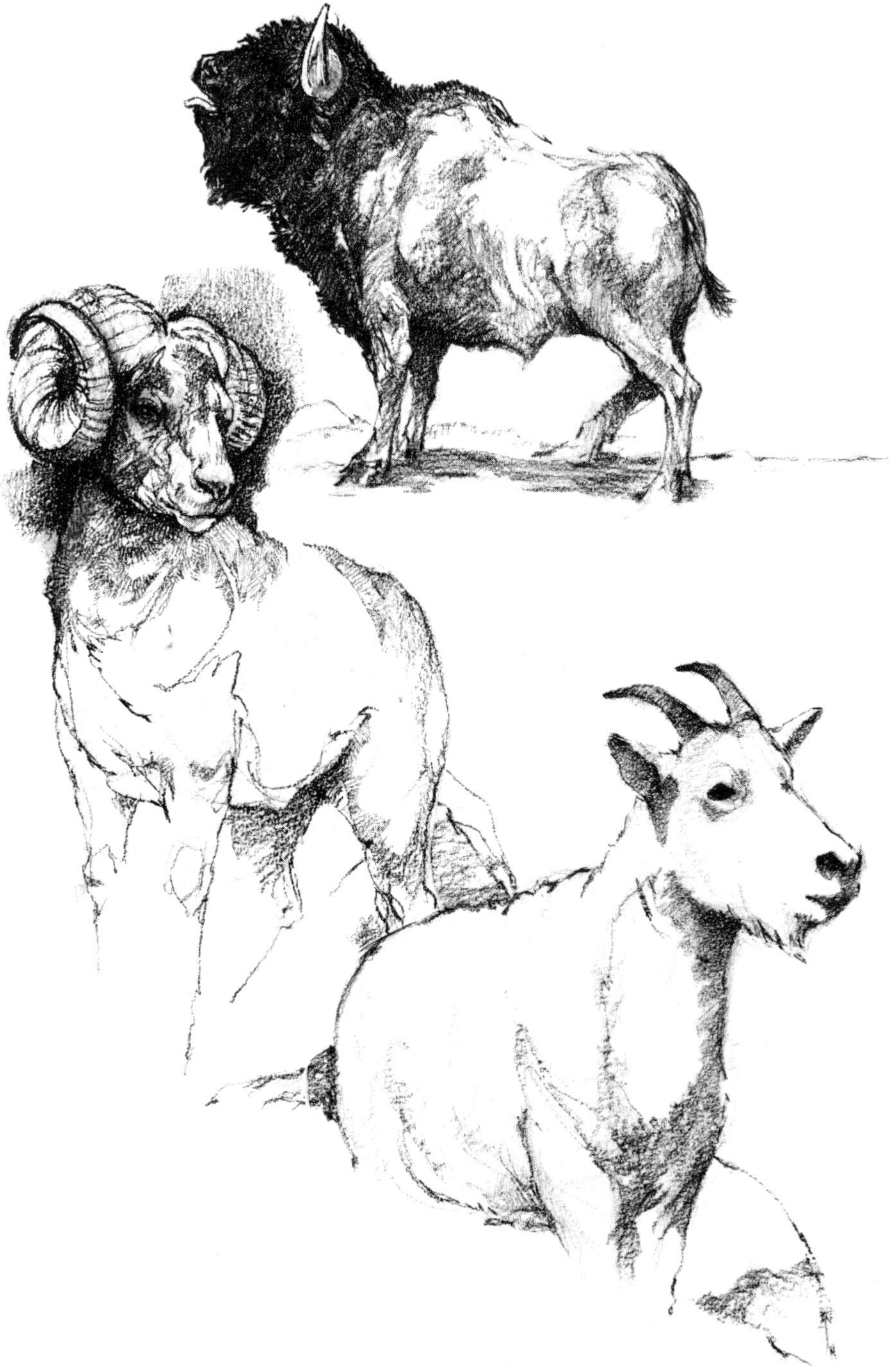

worked on both faces, in characteristic styles depending on time and place, that they begin to have names and tell us something.

Rare until almost 11,000 years ago, these specialized points suddenly become so numerous as to suggest that hunters, long hemmed in behind the ice barrier, at last burst through with the superior weapons they had invented in the Northland. Opposed to this theory, however, is the puzzling fact that the oldest of these points are not found in the North. They seem to be at least as old as far south as South America. Considering their variety and wide distribution, they may go back at least 14,000 years. No doubt they were invented, or developed from simpler forms, by New·World hunters whose mouths watered for more frequent servings of big game. But where this happened remains a mystery. It could have been in two or more places.

Some of the oldest specialized points were found in a cave in the Sandia Mountains near Albuquerque, New Mexico. A Sandia point is shaped like a lance tip except for a shoulder at one corner of the base, where it was attached to the shaft. This is believed to be the form from which that great favorite of the mammoth hunters, the fluted Clovis point, was developed. Fluting, consisting of a channel running from the base toward the tip, served to lighten the weight, especially when applied to both faces.

Though named for a site near Clovis, New Mexico, Clovis points have since been found in even greater numbers all over eastern North America. We can imagine the elephant hunters first being drawn to the southern prairies where the grass was high and the sunflowers tall. Then the glaciers began a slow retreat from the Great Lakes area, and some of the hunters moved northward. Forests took over the land reclaimed from the ice sheets, but there was browse by the streams for the shaggy mastodon, a woodland elephant, and for the deer and the giant beaver. The whole of eastern North America was strewn with Clovis points by 10,000 years ago, giving a perhaps mistaken impression that big-game hunters were the only pioneers to fill this once empty land.

Fluting reached its pinnacle of perfection in the Folsom points of the Plains hunters, of which the famous one removed from the rib cage of a bison near Folsom, New Mexico, is an example. The fluting runs nearly the entire length of these points, making them like hollow shells. So delicately are the edges retouched that the craftsmen who removed the tiny chips must have taken pride in adding beauty to usefulness.

Points were made in many styles: fluted, flaked in parallel ripples, stemmed, notched, triangular, or slim and tapering at both ends like a willow leaf. Hunters thought nothing of walking three days to a quarry for chert, chalcedony, jasper, or petrified wood with the flaking qualities they wanted.

The willow-leaf Cascade point of the Pacific Northwest may be as old as the fluted points. Hunters came into this region looking for deer. At places like Five Mile Rapids on the Columbia, they saw fat salmon leaping upstream, a sight that was to determine the lifeway of their descendants for the next 10,000 years.

Willow-leaf points spread south along the mountains and may or may not have inspired points of similar shape in Mexico and South America. In the absence of boats, the way to South America was necessarily along the full length of the Isthmus of Panama, today a maze of jungle and mangrove swamp. But before the sea rose, it may have been a wide, grassy strip of parkland. Beyond the Isthmus, man could fan out over the Venezuelan grasslands or could follow the great rivers of Colombia into the high valleys of the Andes.

Man had long since passed through the cold filter. Now, 10,000, perhaps 20,000 years ago, he crossed the equator. It was hot on the coast but bone-chilling 13,000 feet up in the Peruvian mountains where, 9,500 years ago, he was tracking deer and guanaco under the brow of receding glaciers. This was summer hunting. Man wintered in the lower valleys, and some of his companions went to the coast for mussels and clams and the wild potatoes that sprang up in the fog-shrouded lowlands.

Ready to fight for a foothold wherever he went, man was like no other animal. He pieced out his diet with snails and berries, flushed tapirs from the thorny underbrush, and tackled ant-eating glyptodons as big as bears. As a predator he outlasted the dire wolf and the saber-toothed cat. The rivals he most respected were the puma and the jaguar. For them he came in time to feel a mystic tie, a sense of religious kinship.

By highland basins man passed into Chile. He fished on the coast or crossed the mountains to the Argentine pampas, where he hurled balls of stone joined by a cord at the legs of camel-like guanacos and ostrich-like rheas. He found the Brazilian highlands pleasing but shunned the Amazon forests. There were fish aplenty in quiet pools by the tropical rivers, but who wanted to wade in among caymans, anacondas, piranhas, and electric eels to get them? This watery world waited till man could exploit it in canoes.

We have seen that man reached the southernmost tip of South America, where the cold forest and tundra were like the terrain his ancestors had traversed at the top of America. Here he hunted not mammoths and caribou but ground sloths, wild horses, and kicking, spitting guanacos that were ill-tempered and indisposed to yield up their flesh.

By 10,000 years ago, man had moved into every corner of the New World from which he could wrest a living with the weapons and wisdom he then commanded. He was not a tribesman in the proper sense of the word but belonged to the simpler society of a band, which, if we may go by more recent examples in various parts of the world, consisted of perhaps thirty to sixty individuals. They considered themselves close kin and usually were. When the hunting and fishing were good, they camped together, helped one another, and shared the food. In lean times, they broke up into separate families and went their own way for a season before reuniting.

A band was in more or less friendly contact with ten or twenty other bands, sharing a common language with them. Good relations were kept up by visiting, exchanging gifts, and holding great feasts. These ties among neighboring bands served to keep the peace and, most important, were a means of finding marriage partners. Marriage between bands fortified traditional friendships, so that even a lone hunter would find hospitable relatives wherever he went.

Marriage customs also fixed a minimum number to the size of a band. Let it dwindle to, say, fifteen members, and a young hunter might go looking for a wife in vain, all because he hadn't an eligible sister or girl cousin to marry into another band. There was a top limit, too, for when a band became too numerous for the local food resources, some had to take off and look for a new homeland. Until that necessity arose, it was better to remain where you knew the deer runs, hickory groves, and fishing streams and work them in their seasons, moving from camp to camp over familiar ground.

If a band killed an elephant, it was not all in the day's work. It was the event of the year. Only as projectile points became sharper and surer was man tempted to abandon his ancient routine and go wandering after the big herd animals, camping at temporary kill sites and watering places, then moving on, perhaps never to return. It was a bold, restless, and very self-confident band that would pull up stakes and accept the risks of specialized big-game hunting. To what extent big-game hunting became the general pattern of life in various regions is in dispute among the authorities. What's certain is that the mammoth and bison hunters left abundant mementos of their stirring new lifeway, in the shape of well-made points and dismembered skeletons. Nowhere have these hunters been so carefully studied as on the Great Plains, and so there we return to see how it went with them in the heyday of hunting.

No ten-ton mammoth could find enough to eat among the clumps of short grass on the arid Plains today. But 11,000 years ago the climate was moist, the grass tall and filling, and tree-lined streams wound between shallow lakes and ponds left by the glaciers. Elephants came to the watering places at their mortal risk, for hunters were lying in wait, their spears tipped with Clovis points three to five inches long and sharp enough to pierce a tough hide. Even so, one hit, or two or three, were not immediately fatal unless they reached the heart or the spinal cord. A daring spearsman might steal up behind the beast's massive foreleg and drive through to a vital spot, but it seems that the usual strategy was to cut a young animal from the herd and, by shouting, feinting, and letting missiles fly, drive it deep into the mire where, helpless, it could be dispatched at leisure. The large boulders found at a Wyoming kill site are more than adequate for delivering the final blows.

The remains of nine mammoths that all died young about 11,260 years ago were found on a ranch in southeastern Arizona beside what was once a freshwater pool. With them lay Clovis points, butchering tools, and such signs of good cheer as roasting hearths and skulls smashed to get at the tongue and brains. But man did not live by elephant alone even in those good days. There were fragments found in Arizona of bison, tapir, and wild horse. And the site at Clovis, New Mexico, reveals that big-game hunters were sometimes reduced to rodents and turtles, or even a wolf.

Poor mammoths, the odds were against them! Unlike rabbits, they did not multiply rapidly. A baby elephant's prenatal life is twice that of man. And with hunters picking off the young by preference, too few of them reached maturity. Perhaps the climate would have done in the mammoths in any case. The ice retreated, advanced, and retreated again in the period between 12,000 and 10,000 years ago, but the trend was unmistakable. As the rains lessened, the grasses and reeds became sparser around the shrinking water holes. Not much later than 11,000 years ago the golden age of the mammoths was over on the Plains. Their woollier relatives in the northern forests gave way to caribou and moose. Of all the American elephants, only the browsing mastodon held out a few millennia longer in the eastern woodlands.

The bison now became king of the Plains, a huge, big-humped bison with flaring horns and a low-slung head that could sweep a foot of snow from the grass with one sideways pass. Folsom points seem to have been designed especially for the pursuit of this magnificent beast. They have been found at the Lindenmeier campsite in northeastern Colorado together with a variety of tools, including knives that were probably attached to handles. Apparently spear-throwers were not yet in use on the Plains, but hunting households were enjoying such adjuncts of gracious living as bone needles with eyes, carved beads, and chunks of red pigment, useful for painting anything from a bison hide to the human body.

Later bison hunters, using other types of points, resorted to extreme measures. Near Plainview, Texas, the bones of a hundred bison were found piled up as if they had been stampeded into a blind alley of some sort, where the leaders were trampled by the onrushing herd. At a site in southeastern Colorado, two hundred bison were stampeded over a cliff to perish, heads or hindquarters up, in the arroyo below. It is astonishing how much of the scene can be reconstructed. The herd was grazing downwind from the arroyo, for otherwise the keen-scented animals would have detected the men on their flanks. That the hunters closed in from both sides is shown by the location of projectile points in the skeletal remains. It was late May or early June, because among the bison were calves a few days old. Only the year is missing, but that can not have been far from 8,500 years ago. The hunting band was numerous, or maybe two or three bands cooperated, for they butchered many animals on a sort of assembly, or disassembly, line, piling up forelegs, shoulder blades, and so on, in separate heaps.

For the hunters it was too good to last. Their very success speeded the extinction of the larger bison, already threatened by growing aridity, and after 8,000 years ago only the smaller buffalo remained. The camel and the American horse did not survive much longer, nor the giant armadillo. The ground sloth disappeared from North America. By 8,000 years ago, if not sooner, the heyday of hunting was over. The pursuit of big game continued on a smaller scale where the buffalo roamed the Plains and the guanaco the pampas. But the mammoth and the big-horned bison were gone forever, and with them a certain life-style. Was man the big-time hunter just another Ice Age animal marked for extinction, or at least for demotion to the status of a forager, scrounging for odds and ends? Or was human ingenuity equal to the task of elaborating new lifeways?

5
Forest and Shore

A SLAB OF STONE, pitted with small cuplike depressions, is one answer to the question of how man made out after the grass withered and the Ice Age animals disappeared. It is a nutting stone. The pits held hickory nuts in place while they were cracked.

The nutting stone is one of various implements reflecting new customs from an excavated rock shelter in southern Illinois. A milling stone, on which seeds were crushed to powder, shows wear from long use. Somewhat younger, and dated at 5000 B.C., is a stone ax, grooved for hafting to a wooden handle. It is a promise of an array of woodworking tools soon to come: axes ground to a fine edge, wedges for splitting timber, adzes for trimming poles and shafts, and gouges for shaping and hollowing logs for dugout canoes.

These tools were not flaked and chipped in the old-fashioned way, but were pecked and pounded into shape, then smoothed to a high polish. Armed with them, a man felt confident in the forest, where hardwoods were replacing the pine and spruce, as those had replaced the grasslands. Hunting ways, too, were changing. When a man went into the brush after deer, alone or with a companion, he carried a spear-thrower and used broad-bladed points, notched at the corners and sure to stay embedded in the flesh. He was prepared to follow a wounded deer two or three days, if necessary, until it collapsed. If no deer came in view, he might return with only a porcupine to be roasted in the hot ashes. It was, at least, a token and spared him the humiliation of subsisting solely on the mussels his wife pried from the stream bank or the turtles his children caught in the pond.

Thus began a new hunting and gathering stage. Known in the eastern United States as the Archaic, it has been described as a lifeway to which big-game hunters resorted by necessity as the Ice Age waned. No doubt many did just that, but the Archaic was already under way in some places before the heyday of hunting was over, so it may in considerable part be the work of simple foragers who shared the New World with the big-game hunters or even preceded them. Latecomers out of the North also may have had a hand in it.

The Archaic and other lifeways of the time marked a supreme effort on man's part to adjust to drastic changes, seemingly for the worse, in his surroundings. In the course of 6,000 years over the expanse of two continents, people made countless adaptations and came out, on the whole, ahead. There is space to describe here only some outstanding examples of the various ways they did it.

The Archaic lifeway, simple at first, becomes richly inventive as it unfolds. Along watercourses in Tennessee and Kentucky, great heaps of mussel shells accumulated for more than 2,000 years, starting about 5000 B.C. The climate was warm, the streams were shallow, and shellfish were easy to gather. Freshwater fish were taken with bone fishhooks and nets of twisted plant fiber. Beaver and otter were about, besides squirrels in the oak groves and deer in the forest clearings. To bring his spear-thrower into better balance, man weighted it with a polished and sculptured bannerstone. He brought down deer not only for venison but also to obtain bone and antler for tools, sinew for tough cordage, and leather for clothing. He made awls and needles for his wife's sewing and basketwork and gave her animal teeth to be strung as beads. A bear's incisor was a brave man's proof of true devotion. The dead were buried with democratic simplicity, their legs flexed to fit into a round pit. The burial offerings were simple, nothing splendid enough for a great chief or a king. After 3500 B.C., surprisingly, dogs were buried in the same fashion and sometimes with their masters — a sign that they were regarded more as friends than as food. How dogs reached Tennessee no one knows, but they must have been introduced from the North after being domesticated perhaps in Alaska or Siberia. Hunting dogs appeared, in America at least, when man settled down and needed help in hunting nonmigratory small game. Polished stone cooking vessels, tedious to make and heavy to carry, are another indication of man's having a more or less permanent home, from which he went out in search of food, or even to trade, but to which he returned.

Conch shells from Florida and copper pins, needles, and ornaments from the Upper Great Lakes were reaching Kentucky by 2500 B.C., presumably through trade channels. Man had moved into Wisconsin and the Lake Superior region as the ice retreated, and by 3000 B.C. — some say much earlier — he was breaking native copper from its outcrops with fire and water and, by hammering and grinding, making it into knives, spearheads, harpoon points, ax heads, fishing gear, needles, bracelets, beads, and pendants. He understood annealing, that is, heating and chilling copper by turns to render it less brittle. He hunted with dogs as small as terriers and as large as huskies. He fished and handled a canoe. No one could get around in this land of lakes without boating skills. It could have been the descendants of the copper-using pioneers who invented the light, sturdy, beautiful birchbark canoe.

Over most of the New World, man was becoming a fish-eater and devising the means to satisfy his appetite. He used a deer-bone fishhook or a gorge that turned crosswise at a pull of the line. He built traps, spread nets to which floats and sinkers were attached, or waded after his prey with a three-pronged fish spear. He fished in fresh water and salt water. One of his most remarkable undertakings has been discovered in Boston. Dating from 2500 B.C. and now called the Boylston Street Fish Weir, it consisted of 65,000 sharp stakes driven into the tideland. Brush was packed between the stakes, thus completing a fence that let the ebb tide pass but blocked the fish, leaving them stranded on the beach. What sort of a community the fishermen lived in we do not know, but there must have been many of them working together the year around just to keep so ambitious a project in repair.

By 2000 B.C. the California Indians, hailing from many other places as Californians still do, were tired of grumbling in their scores of languages over their meager diet of shellfish and seeds and struck out on new lifeways. Acorn meal became the staff of life in California's oak-mantled central valleys, once a means was found to remove the bitter taste. Ingenious women did it by letting warm water trickle repeatedly through the pounded nutmeats. They baked the meal as bread or boiled it as mush, using a leak-proof woven basket and dropping in heated stones. One may wonder what part the men had in this acorn-meal economy. They climbed the trees and shook the acorns loose while the women gathered them in baskets.

The men played a more valiant role along the coast. On Santa Catalina Island, twenty miles off the California shore, a refuse heap dated at 1900 B.C. bears evidence that by then boatmen were spearing porpoises, seals, and dolphins in the open sea.

Man's readiness to venture away from the shore is also made evident by the presence of the bones of deep-sea fish in mounds along the Peruvian coast. Similar refuse heaps in Ecuador have yielded female figurines of stone and clay, as well as shards of bowls and jars, the earliest New World pottery of which we know. It dates from 3200 B.C. and is too well made for beginners' work. Ceramic experts liken its grooved and dotted decorative pattern to that of Japan of the same period and propose the idea that the pottery art was introduced by Japanese fishermen who were blown off their course and carried by winds and currents to Ecuador. Other specialists are mystified but unconvinced.

Still more refuse heaps have been explored along the coast of Venezuela and the Guianas. In them were found bone points for fish spears and gouges of hard, tough shell, once used as canoe-making tools, along with remains of snared and netted birds, lobsters, fish and shellfish, rabbits, and occasionally an anteater or a peccary. By 2000 B.C., canoemen from these shores were in the West Indies, blown there by accident at first, perhaps, but later making planned voyages and so rounding out man's occupation of the New World.

Shell mounds continue down the Atlantic coast of Brazil and into the Amazon Basin. It's hard to tell how man gained his living in the steaming interior 3,000 or 4,000 years ago, for the evidence lies buried in forest litter or has rotted away. But we imagine he was most at home in his canoe, spearing fish, manatees, and river dolphins or stepping ashore on the shady side to gather turtle eggs. When he pushed through vines and creepers into the forest, he heard monkeys howling in the upper tier of branches, but they were almost always beyond his reach even if he shinnied up the tall, unbranched trunks. The tree sloth, clinging upside down to a favorite limb, was more accessible only in appearance, for red fire ants swarmed in the tree, reconciled to the sloth but not to intruding man.

There were palm fruits to be gathered in more open country, and wild honey, but on the whole man found it more convenient to stay by the river and club a crocodile or float in among the ducks in a pond, his face covered with a calabash, and grab a bird or two by the legs. There was too much driftwood in the great rivers for net fishing, but poisons made from various vines and stems and dropped into quiet pools would stupefy the fish and bring them to the surface.

Quite likely the shaman conducted a ceremony to show proper respect to the great fish spirit for the first catch of the season. This is a widespread custom that has survived in tropical South America and may go back to early times. Another was the ant ordeal, which required a boy reaching puberty to prove his manhood by submitting to painful ant bites without complaint. A girl, for her part, went into retreat, drinking through a bird-bone tube and scratching herself with a stick instead of her nails. And a man, upon becoming a father, took to his hammock as if he shared the pains of labor and was insisting that fathers are important too.

The fathers who felt most insecure must have been the frustrated canoemen who hunted sea lions in the icy channels of the archipelago off Chile's far southern coast. Here, for man, was the end of the world, a wind-swept land of cool summers and sleety winters, where a fur cape was a luxury and a coat made from grass the usual protection against the elements. The hunting was so poor here that each family went about alone, mostly by water. Canoe nomads, they have been called, carrying their fire with them on the clay-coated floors of their boats, along with the poles and skin coverings they used for setting up temporary quarters on shore.

Since sea lions were scarce, a man's best chance was to club one sleeping on the shore. He might also paddle out at night with a torch and lay hands on a drowsy cormorant or two where they roosted on the rocks. Two things kept the family from starvation. The children, as soon as they could toddle, were sent out at low tide to gather sea urchins. And their mother dived for mussels in the icy water, holding a bag between her teeth.

It was a great day when someone came upon a beached whale, for then people from miles around gathered to feast and sing and dance. It would have been a good time to hold the traditional mock battle between the sexes, though we cannot be sure that this curious custom, by which the men bolstered their self-esteem, may not date from later times. It was the ceremonial reenactment, in part, of an ancient story. Once upon a time, it seems, the women, by their cunning and witchcraft, cruelly lorded it over the men. But at last their cowed husbands, unable to stand any more, resorted to counter-magic. They formed a men's society with a secret ritual. Bloodcurdling shrieks issued from their lodge, and spirit impersonators went forth in hideous costumes, pursuing the women and not relenting until they had frightened them into proper submission to their sea-hunter husbands.

It is interesting to compare these bleak, impoverished islands with the rain-drenched shoreline that extends from northern California to southern Alaska. Both regions have forests of needle-bearing trees and are characterized by headlands, estuaries, narrows, half-drowned valleys, and island mazes. But whereas the frigid waters off the south Chilean coast were poor in marine life, the Pacific Northwest, bathed by warm ocean currents, was infinitely richer in opportunities for food-gathering man.

Long ago, as we have seen, hunters had come down to the Northwest Coast, looking for deer but staying to catch salmon. More people kept coming, especially after 2000 B.C., over the passes from the Plateau, down the great rivers like the Fraser and the Columbia, and perhaps along the coast from Alaska. They introduced polished stone tools and new weapons, including the toggle harpoon, which, with its line and detachable head, let a good marksman play a seal as if it were a fish. Some of the new food-gathering techniques that appeared in the Northwest and even in the Northeast may have been inspired, if not actually imported, from Siberia, not over the now inundated land bridge, of

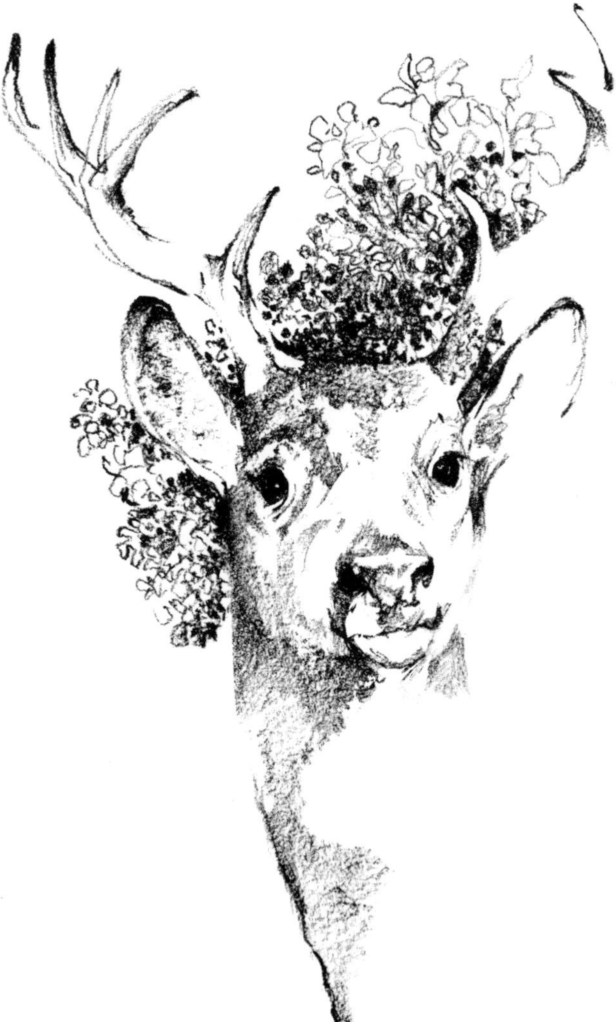

course, but in water craft carrying nomad seal hunters and even traders and migrants across the Bering Strait.

The Pacific Northwest abounded in seafood: clams, octopi, smelt, cod, oily oulachon that would burn like a candle, halibut that weighed as much as a man, and salmon that leaped the rapids and waterfalls in the spawning season. Hungry seals followed the salmon runs from the salt water into the fresh. Minks and bears waited upstream for fish, competing with man's nets and weirs. But there was salmon enough for all, and man was confident they'd come back inexhaustibly if he showed his respect and returned the bones to the sea. The problem was not so much how to take the fish as how to preserve them. As the fishermen hauled them in, the women toiled unceasingly, splitting and cleaning them to be dried or smoked.

The rule for all foods was to use them in season: green sprouts in early spring, bulbs in May, berries in summer and fall, waterfowl during their twice-yearly migrations. But it was important to save for later on. So they learned to dry some of the blackberries and rendered the salmon fat into oil to store it in vessels made of seal bladders. By 1000 B.C. the foresighted people of the Northwest were making efficient use of their homeland's varied resources. Still better times were coming, but for then it was a good life.

A comparable stage was reached in the eastern United States between 2000 B.C. and 1000 B.C. Techniques had been perfected for making full use of each region's resources. Deer, elk, and bear were highly esteemed, but lesser game also was systematically hunted and trapped: rabbits, squirrels, raccoons, opossums, otters, porcupines, groundhogs, turkeys, wildfowl, and fish. Several hundred plants, including their roots, stalks, stems, leaves, buds, and fruits, were used as foods, medicines, dyes, or textile fibers. Polished stone tools with stout handles were available for exploiting the forests and making wooden utensils and boats. Despite the passing of the big game, the population, as estimated from wigwam sites and burial plots, was several times larger than when the mastodon crashed through the young postglacial forest. The Wapanucket site in Massachusetts was already, in 2300 B.C., enough of a village to have six roomy lodges, a council house, cremation pits, and a mortuary where the ashes of the departed and the implements needed

for a long journey were sprinkled with powdered red ocher.

By projecting back from what we know of later Indian hunters, we can at least imagine what growing up was like a millennium or so before Christ. Children were not punished much except by being told edifying tales of the crow that was too greedy or the fox that was too crafty for its own good. Whenever they acquired an adult skill, they had many, many relatives to praise them. A boy learned to work in wood, antler, bone, and stone and to equip himself with a far more specialized set of tools than his ancestors had known. He could put a high polish on a stone bead and drill a hole through it by feeding sand and water to the point of the instrument. He practiced setting spring-pole traps, building deadfalls, stalking in disguise, and blowing imitation moose calls on a bark trumpet. If a moose came, he was ready, let's say with his spear-thrower, for scholars do not agree on just when the bow and arrow reached the United States. The boy had been taught to address the moose courteously, dead or alive, as "Grandfather." Upon killing his first large animal, he gave all the meat to his aged relatives. This was to teach him generosity. But he had his reward. He was now mature enough to consider marrying.

His sister gathered shellfish, greens, and wild fruit in their seasons and crushed roots and nutmeats. From her mother — or from her aunts, who were also "mothers" in some languages — she learned to cook in an earth oven, wrapping the morsels in green leaves and burying them in a pit with hot stones several hours before mealtime. Boiling was made easy after pottery cooking vessels appeared, as they did in Georgia and Florida about 2000 B.C. and later — sometimes much later — in other places. Whether this or that pottery type diffused from South America and Mexico, or from Asia, or was the work of home talent, is still under debate. But whatever the origins of pottery types, there is much to admire in the achievements of early woman, who arranged her coiffure with bone hairpins and a comb, sewed moccasins and buckskin garments, stowed away skin bags of pemmican, and wove baskets, sleeping mats, and nets. She could also finger-weave a cloth of sorts, and it would be picturesque to show her at a simple loom, but she probably did not know of its existence, though it may have been used by this time in Mexico and certainly was in Peru.

One thing we shouldn't project back to these times is organized warfare. There must have been skirmishes over berry patches and women, but each band had a stake in keeping the peace with neighbors among whom they had relatives and in-laws and with whom they shared pleasant memories of feasting and dancing. Rather than start a feud, it was better to punish a fellow band member who had gone looking for trouble. During great migrations there were intruders to resist, flee from, or learn to live with, but such occasions were not frequent. The time of warrior tribesmen looking for plunder and brave deeds to recite was not yet come. The bands were too scattered, too small and leaderless. What was gathered was soon consumed, and little remained for others to covet. America consisted of small groups hard at work in a homeland they knew intimately and in which they lived frugally and even austerely but in reasonable peace and contentment.

6
Eskimo Lifeways

It would simplify our story to say that the Eskimos were the last non-Europeans to come to America. But that statement raises questions easier to ask than to answer:

When *did* they come? And who were they?

Eskimos weren't Indians in the usual sense. That in itself doesn't tell us much, since for lack of better information we tend to bunch the earlier comers together as Indians, though the very earliest of them, to judge by their skeletons, might not pass as Indians today.

Most Indians, however, carry a Mongoloid imprint, some more and some less. With Eskimos there is no doubt. They are strongly Mongoloid. As far back as the record goes, they bear a closer resemblance to Asians across the Bering Strait than to their nearest Indian neighbors. The broad Eskimo face, with its low nose and pads of fat, may have been inherited from the coldest times of the last glaciation, as nature's way of protecting the sinuses and breathing passages from the sharp, dry Siberian air.

This explanation fits in with the theory that the Indians, or many of them, came to America early and escaped these extreme rigors of climate. If they arrived before the way south was blocked by ice, then for thousands of years, so the reasoning goes, they were shut off from contact with the Asian ancestors of the Eskimos. The latter, when they came, brought their Eskimo physical traits, including type-B blood, which was foreign to Indians, as we have seen, but fairly common among Eskimos and the related Aleuts. Linguistic studies indicate that these two peoples spoke a common Eskimo-Aleut language until about 2600 B.C. Even today, it is said, an Eskimo from northwest Alaska can understand one from Greenland, three thousand miles away.

On the face of it, why not assume that the Eskimos were Asian hunters who, not many thousand years ago, climbed into their skin boats, huddled in parkas, and paddled over the Bering Strait to an Alaskan beachhead, from which they gradually dispersed, pursuing

Eskimos

the seal and the walrus, across the top of North America? This, more or less, was the story of the Eskimos as told a generation ago. Since then, new discoveries have shown that into the making of the Eskimos went various peoples who met and mixed down the centuries and borrowed one another's customs. At some time, of course, a wave of migrants must have brought an Eskimo language to America, but scholars are far from agreed on when that was. In any case, the Eskimo-speakers joined with those who were already there and together they made the best of their harsh surroundings. All the while, new ideas kept filtering in from various parts of North America and Asia. The new lifeways that emerged were not based on the forest and tundra alone but reached out and exploited the animals that swam in northern seas and under the Arctic ice.

Before there were Eskimos, other men, as we know, had reached Alaska and northern Canada. Some passed on south, others found themselves locked behind the great ice barrier or were content to remain in the north for the good hunting on the tundra. Their culture, not surprisingly, was more Asian than American. In fact, while the land bridge existed, the Northland was geographically part of Siberia. Its hunting weapons, in contrast to those farther south, reveal a closer, more immediate relationship to northern Asia ("immediate" here meaning a couple of thousand years or so). This influence stands out clearly after 8000 or 9000 B.C. with the appearance of little stone blades, an inch or so long, that archaeologists call microblades. They served as tips for bone points or were fitted into slots along the sides of bone and antler projectile heads. Such weapons produced a jagged, bleeding wound and were increasingly used in the Old World and the New as the ice retreated and game grew scarcer.

These microblades, along with highly skilled bone-working techniques, were known in Siberia and Japan before they reached Alaska, presumably by way of the land bridge. When we say that the land bridge is no more, an exception should perhaps be made for the easternmost of the Aleutian Islands, which, during the Ice Age, were joined to the Alaska Peninsula. One of them, tiny Anangula, is believed to have stood at a bend of the southern shore that was brushed by ocean currents moving into the Bering Sea. Samples of charcoal, taken from among the stone blades, large and small, at a campsite there, gave a radiocarbon date of 6400 B.C., but man may have come earlier, while the land bridge was still intact. In any case, he found himself in a seafood paradise, and his descendants developed fishing and sealing skills that helped form the Eskimo way of life.

At low tide, the small children of Anangula could gather sea urchins on the beach, while their older brothers pried octopi out of crevices in the reefs. We see their father taking fish with a dip net and wading to an offshore rookery for cormorant and puffin eggs, safe there from foxes but not from man. Harbor seals hauled up on shore in the breeding season, but fur seals swam by on their migrations, out of reach perhaps but not out of sight. Their appearance must have been a stimulus to navigation. The kayak was a swift, skin-covered craft that a man could carry to the beach, launch in the surf, and handle in a stormy sea while wielding a harpoon. Just when the kayak was perfected is not known, but it reached its highest development in the Aleutians. Along with the umiak, which required a crew of eight or ten, it made the larger fish and mammals of northern seas available as food for man and became part of the heritage shared by Aleuts and Eskimos.

Among hunters farther north, the story unfolded in other ways. After the mammoth was gone, they pursued caribou on the tundra and bison on the grasslands spreading in the wake of the melting ice. Their ranks probably were enlarged by big-game hunters pushing in from the Plains and elsewhere. By 5000 B.C. the climate had warmed so much that birch and spruce forests were spreading over the northern grasslands and deep into the tundra. It was bad news for the caribou hunters to have trees screening their favorite prey from sight. During the spring and fall migrations, they could wait, of course, at a stream crossing and spear the milling, swimming animals. But between these happy times there were months when even a snowy owl was a treat.

It became imperative to supplement a caribou diet

with other game, and so a new lifeway developed in the inland woods and waters of northwestern Canada and Alaska. It is reflected in a versatile tool collection that seems to be drawn from sources near at hand and as far away as northern Asia. Besides a wide assortment of burins and microblades for working bone and antler and arming weapons, there are adzes for felling trees, beaver-tooth gouges for hollowing out trunks for dugout canoes, net sinkers, and barbed antler spears for taking lake fish. This equipment and a combination of summer fishing with winter hunting assured the livelihood of a people who looked more Mongoloid than most Indians but were nevertheless destined to be Indians. They had departed from the line of development that was leading to the Eskimos.

There was another answer to the caribou crisis — a bold Eskimo answer — but it meant going to a stormy land's end where noisy ice floes grind and crash, or, resting in sheltered bays, pile up in thick ceilings through which imprisoned seals must break winter breathing holes. During the centuries around 3000 B.C., a sorting out was going on between the forest Indians and the pre-Eskimos of the coastlands and tundra. The Eskimos, it is true, continued to trek inland after caribou, and the Indians, particularly along more southern coasts, went after sea mammals. Nevertheless, the tree line became more or less a frontier, Indians to the south, Eskimos to the north.

Soon after 3000 B.C., early signs of an Eskimo lifeway

began appearing in western Alaska, both north and south of the Bering Strait. The trend quickened as the climate cooled somewhat around 2200 B.C. and the tundra reclaimed ground from the forest. Because of its burins, microblades, and needle-like engraving tools, this lifeway is linked to what is known as the Arctic Small Tool tradition. Microblades were nothing new, but now they were flaked and edged with jewel-like precision. They served as side blades and end blades for spears and harpoons and were set in bone handles and used for scraping hides. Similar blades and burins have been found in the Lena River Valley of Siberia and the Gobi Desert of Mongolia, but the Small Tool tradition seems to have come to full flower in America following a sizable Mongoloid migration across the Bering Strait from somewhere in Asia.

The newcomers were not exactly Eskimos and they may or may not have spoken an Eskimo tongue. But in terms of what they brought with them, what they borrowed by mixing with their predecessors, and what they learned in the hard school of the seal and walrus hunt, they heralded the full Eskimo culture of later times. As yet they lacked tight winter houses. The typical oval outline of their camping places on beaches and promontories, strewn with flint chips and fire-cracked pebbles, suggests that they lived in skin-covered, dome-shaped huts where they stone-boiled their meat in birch baskets and flaked the weapons that procured it. These weapons included some of the earliest arrowheads known in America, consisting of slender rods of antler or walrus ivory, tipped with stone sharp and thin enough to pierce a caribou to the heart. Apparently the toggle-head harpoon was already in use, its detachable head swiveling and tightening in the flesh of the quarry at a tug of the retrieving line. No adversary was more formidable than the hulking walrus, who summered on an ice floe and dived for starfish, scraping them from the ocean floor with his incredibly long tusks, which were equally useful as supports when he heaved his two tons of flesh and blubber back onto his resting place. The man who harpooned a walrus had to sit tight in his little skin boat, and he needed thick mittens to protect his hands when the bewhiskered sea mammal took off in fury with the spinning line.

This lifeway, or variations of it, spread from Alaska to the rocky islands and peninsulas of the Canadian Arctic and at length reached the coasts of Greenland, Labrador, and Newfoundland. It was more a spread of ideas and skills than of great masses of people. Arctic hunters, as far back as we know them, have been loosely attached to their bands and have felt free to move on with their families, hoping for better luck. Knowledge of new weapons, therefore, passed quickly from camp to camp in the gossip of travelers and visitors.

As the company warmed their hands at a driftwood fire on the beach, there often must have been brave talk of the whale herds that came swimming poleward in

April as leads opened in the ice. Each whale was as long as ten men were tall and carried between his head and his flukes enough flesh, fat, and oil to turn famine into weeks of plenty. Yet for centuries the whale, unless beached and stinking, remained an impossible dream. To harpoon a two-ton walrus was no mean feat, and a bowhead whale weighed sixty tons. Even if a hunter ventured close enough to drive his stone point home, even if the line of walrus hide held without snapping, the mighty leviathan, upon sounding, would draw the frail craft and all aboard into the depths of the cold sea.

Some 1800 years before Christ these obstacles were overcome. A band of hunters, by their courage, ingenuity, and superb teamwork, mastered the art of capturing the whale. Known to us as the Old Whaling people, they lived on a beach on Cape Krusenstern in northwestern Alaska. Since the time when they scanned the horizon for the whale parade, new beaches have been raised by wind and wave. Today what remains of their village of five half-underground winter houses and five bark-roofed summer lodges is a mile inland.

This site where the Old Whaling people kept their vigil has yielded any number of whale jaws, skulls, ribs, and vertebrae — so many of the latter that they were set around for use as chairs. Here on a house floor is a lance blade eight inches long and here a harpoon head a hand's breadth wide. These are clearly large weapons intended for whale. For the rest of the picture we must look to later times and suppose that whale hunting was much the same in 1800 B.C.

Imagine we are eight, the crew of an umiak. When the whales come, six will be at the paddles, three on each side. The helmsman will be in the stern with the steering paddle. In the bow will be the man with the surest aim and the strongest nerve, the harpooner. He is all but fearless, and so should we be, but who is free of apprehension on the eve of a foray that may cost us our lives or the shame of returning empty-handed? So we eight have been communing together, apart from women, whose magic is theirs, not ours. We have purified ourselves in a ritual too secret to describe. We have put on new garments, covered the umiak with new skins, and stowed the gear. Now we wait on the beach. We sing our magic songs to bid the whale come. He hears us.

Presently a black head breaks the surface of the water. We leap to our stations and paddle with all our strength, the helmsman guiding us toward the moving sea monster. The harpooner sings ardently over his weapons. We come close, very close, and he takes aim and plants a broad blade into the half-submerged back of the quarry. The wounded animal sounds. He would carry us, umiak and all, down in his plunge if the line became tangled. We watch it and make sure that all the inflated sealskins attached to it clear the gunwales. These floats act as a drag, impeding the whale's movements and wasting his strength. When he surfaces, the harpooner strikes again, and again, until several lines, each with its floats, are restraining the great beast. As he grows weak from internal bleeding, the fighting mood leaves him, but he thrashes in pain, and a slap of his fluke could capsize us. Cautiously we push the prow onto the whale's very head. The harpooner seizes his killing lance and stabs the doomed animal in the heart, in the lungs, wherever he can.

When the whale is quite dead, we tow the carcass to the shore. The women are waiting for us, our wives, sisters, mothers. It is their turn now. A stately matron offers fresh water to the dead whale, knowing he must be thirsty, poor creature, after so long in the briny deep. Then, as soon as his head is cut off so that his spirit can go free, she makes a courteous little speech, asking him to tell the other whales that he was well treated and that they will be welcome too. Now the carcass can be divided. The women part the flesh with their crescent-shaped stone knives and put aside fair shares for us all. For many nights we shall visit one another, gorging on whale meat, and there will be plenty left over for each family in the village to fill a cache in the frozen ground against the uncertain future.

For all our imagining, the Old Whaling people remain something of a mystery. Their flint chipping does not seem to be in the main line of Eskimo development, and they disappear and go we know not where.

But they were the first we know of who pitted human intelligence and will against the strength of the largest of animals, and the Eskimos who were to come followed their example.

We move on to 1000 B.C., still in northwestern Alaska. Soapstone lamps appear at sites of this date, shallow vessels in which a flame was kept alive, fed by whale oil or seal oil drawn to the end of a moss wick. Two lamps would serve for cooking, warming the interior of a well-insulated sod house, and dissipating the gloom of a long Arctic night. Round-bottomed clay pots bearing stamped designs, ivory harpoons with fineline engraving and polished slate blades, ingenious fishing gear, and blunted arrowheads for stunning birds also make their appearance. With some assurance, scholars speak of the makers of these things as Eskimos. They are not yet the Eskimos who will travel on snowshoes and dog-drawn sleds, with goggles to shield their eyes from the white glare of the snow, but they are the forerunners of such men.

At sites dating from later centuries, the growth of an Eskimo lifeway may be traced along Alaska's western coast and on the easternmost tip of Siberia and the islands of the Bering Sea. Many of its features spread across the Arctic and flowed back, in altered form, to their point of origin. The Eskimo heritage is a fusion of many elements, some formed in the struggle with a hostile climate, others borrowed from the Great Lakes, the Plains, British Columbia, the Aleutians, and Asia.

From the Ice Age onward, the ancestors of the Eskimos absorbed ideas and people from the Old World far more than did other Americans, but they put their own stamp on what they received. The result was an Eskimo lifeway, or rather a number of lifeways, all dedicated to the pursuit of cold-climate game but differing in details. In southern Alaska, the whale was hunted with a poisoned harpoon and left to drift ashore. In the central Arctic, building blocks of ice took the place of turf and stone. And on Greenland's northern tip, not far from the Pole, Eskimos dwelt in such isolation, disputing for seals with polar bears, that until the Europeans came they imagined themselves the only people in the world.

On one thing all Eskimos were agreed, and that was that matrimony was a blessed state. A woman could no more live without a hunter to feed the family than a man could do without a seamstress, to prepare his undergarments with the hair turned in and his outer garments with the fur turned out. He also looked to his wife for his puffin-skin parka with its wolfskin ruff and his watertight fur boots with soles of seal hide, which, wearing her teeth away, she chewed to make pliable. Every stitch with needle and sinew she took with the greatest of care, for it her husband went out into the terrible cold with a gaping seam, she would soon be a widow.

Ties with kinsmen and neighbors were close, for the well-being of all depended on the sharing of game and the happy times people spent together, eating, joking, dancing, and impersonating birds and animals. They lived in small camps without an organized government and for the most part in peace. If a high-spirited young man was tempted in a burst of rage to strike down his enemy, he took second thought, remembering that he needed the good opinion of the group. It was better to settle the dispute in a wrestling match. If the young man was not a good wrestler, he might challenge his adversary to a song duel. Then the two of them would take turns insulting each other, making up clever verses as they went along, and the one who gained the most applause would be acclaimed the winner.

A man spent most of his energy, though, paddling a kayak, fishing through the river ice, hunting caribou on the tundra muck, or lying on a floe, wriggling silently toward a seal's breathing hole. His wife packed in seal oil the sea birds he brought her, hung the fish on drying racks, and filled the underground freezing compartments with flesh and blubber. It was necessary to take and put away as much meat as possible while the sun was shining, for a family of Eskimo size would eat several tons of it during the long night that began in November and lasted till February.

The hunting continued, under difficulties, by the light of the moon and stars, for provisions could always run short. Winter, moreover, was a time for feasting with neighbors in rooms dimly lit by seal-oil lamps. And the long, dark months would have been unbearably dreary without at least one demonstration of the shaman's power to fly to the moon or to visit Sedna at the bottom of the sea and plead for the return of the game.

Sedna was one of the supernatural beings who, at various times and places, have governed the animals that were man's sustenance. While young she had married a seagull. This was not extraordinary, considering how easily animals took human shape and vice versa. The tragedy was that Sedna had been lured to the land of the birds with the promise that she should sleep on soft bearskins and that her lamp should always be filled with oil and her pot with meat. This was a great deceit. She found herself shivering in the snow that sifted into her hut of torn fishskins. So when her father visited her, she fled with him in his boat. But her seagull husband gave pursuit, joined by his fellows. Rending the air with cries of lament, they beat up such a storm that the boat began to sink. To placate them, the terrified father cast his daughter into the water and when, in desperation, she clung to the edge of the boat, he hacked at her fingers to make her let go. The first joints fell into the water and became seals, the second joints, walruses, and the stumps, whales.

Sedna sank into the watery depths and began a new life as mistress of the sea mammals. It was not entirely happy, for the people whom she graciously provided with game were careless of the food tabus. Somewhere a woman would cook seal and caribou meat in the same pot, and this would set up a terrible itching in Sedna's hair. The worst, of course, was that, having no fingers, she could not scratch. All she could do was shut up her animals from thoughtless mankind.

In this situation lay the shaman's opportunity to mediate between the human and spirit worlds. He ordered the lamps put out in the meeting place. To the beat-beat of tambourines, he called on the people to confess their offenses against Sedna's creatures. This done, he summoned his spirit helpers, who came howling and screaming and knocking against the pots. Presently the shaman went into a state of ecstasy and was off in spirit on his mission. He was gone a long time, but when he returned, spent and limp, he brought good tidings. He had told Sedna that the people faced hunger and were sorry they had broken the food tabus.

He had scratched her itching head and combed out her hair. She had relented in her anger and would let the seals and walruses come, willing, even eager, to be eaten by man. And in April, always assuming proper respect from man, there might be the whales.

7
The Desert People

O<small>F ALL THE FIRST</small> A<small>MERICANS</small>, the most wretched were those who scoured the desert for something to eat. They were not there by choice. The desert had crept up on them. Their ancestors had come into the Great Basin as hunters while the Ice Age was waning. Lakes then covered half of Utah and Nevada. Even after horses and camels became extinct, waterfowl abounded: mud hens, grebes, herons, geese, ducks, and their eggs. Small stone points and fragments of shafts show that, as time went on, light darts for throwing at birds replaced heavy spears. Suckers and chub were taken from the lakes in nets of bulrush fiber or in basketry traps.

The water level was down by 7000 B.C., and lower still by 6000 B.C., but who noticed any difference in a lifetime? Eventually, though, the lakes were transformed into marshes and grasslands. They supported small antelope herds and many rabbits, but roots and seeds became the everyday fare. When Danger Cave in Utah was excavated some years ago, pickleweed chaff lay there a dozen feet deep; it was what was left when the seeds were parched, milled, and made into mush.

Caves like this, emerging as the lakes receded, offered man shelter from the blazing sun and the chilly nights of a mountain-hemmed land shut off from tempering sea breezes. Mixed with the litter beneath the floors are such reminders of a seed-gathering way of life as pieces of basketry and slabs of stone.

Seeds as tiny as those of wild grasses were swept into the wide mouths of conical baskets and then winnowed in basketry trays. There were also flat baskets in which seeds were shaken with hot embers until parched, and other baskets for storing a supply for winter. The earliest baskets were made of twined rushes. Later, willow splints were coiled, layer on layer, and firmly tied. Some baskets were tight enough to hold liquids for stone boiling, others were smeared inside and out with pitch and used as water jugs.

The hard, dry seeds of the desert were crushed on a stone slab with the aid of a handstone. The continual rolling back and forth wore a trough in the slab, which evolved in time into a metate or milling stone. Pine nutmeats, being soft, were ground to a paste in a mortar and pestle.

Pine-nut paste and pickleweed porridge go down better when eaten with fish and fowl. But these tastier foods were not easy to come by. Some authorities believe that after 5000 B.C there occurred two or three thousand years of unusual heat and drought. The grass shriveled, the lakes shrank to saline marshes, and the Great Basin became a dreadful place in which to live and work. Others question whether the climate became much worse than it already had been. It certainly did not get better, and the ensuing period, lasting until nearly 2000 B.C., is known, not only in the Basin but in the Southwest and Mexico, as a Desert culture.

The desert people suffered a double disadvantage. They shared the misfortune of all New World hunters in that the Ice Age monsters were long since gone. They also lacked a compensating means of livelihood as generous as the small game of the eastern woodlands, the salmon of the Northwest Coast, or the seals of the Arctic. Small game on the desert meant the jackrabbit, the pocket gopher, the cactus mouse, the kangaroo rat, the sagebrush vole, or insect larvae skimmed from brackish pools.

Of course the desert, at this time, was more than salt flats and shifting dunes. It was the narrow valleys between the Basin ranges, where the minimal rainfall ran off in dry washes, spread out in shallow playas, and evaporated without reaching the sea. It was also the higher mountain slopes, cloaked in juniper, pinyon pine, and spruce, the scattered oases lower down, and the cottonwoods along the streams. A thicket of feathery green mesquite lining a dry bed meant there was water underground. The sign of the waterless desert floor was sagebrush, monotonously spaced as far as the eye could reach.

Cactus thrived in the Basin only if well sheltered from cold winters and dry summers. Its real home was farther south, in the Arizona and Sonora deserts or on the Texas plains and the high plateaus of Mexico. It took countless forms, tiny as a pincushion, big as a tree, or barrel-like with bristling fishhook spines. It branched out in pulpy pads or rose in tall columns that waited only for a thunderstorm to siphon up a few tons of water. Cacti shared the desert with thorny acacias, yuccas with leaves like bayonets and clusters of creamy flowers, and century plants whose leaf tips could be broken off with the fiber attached to serve the desert people as needles and thread.

Plants had needles, serpents had fangs, and the scorpion a stinging tail. This parched and broken land was not a cozy place where one camped by a stream and lived on freshwater clams. Life in the desert was an unending pilgrimage in search of uncertain food. What went into the stomach was paid for with sore feet. For protection from rocks and thorns, the wanderers rubbed their soles with pine pitch or wore sandals of braided sagebrush bark. Buried in the dust of dry caves are sandals that have lasted up to 9,000 radiocarbon-dated years. The tattered footgear found at various levels serves as a clock, letting us know, for example, that some desert bands had dogs by 4000 B.C. They were not yet hunting companions, the experts suspect, but rather a food reserve.

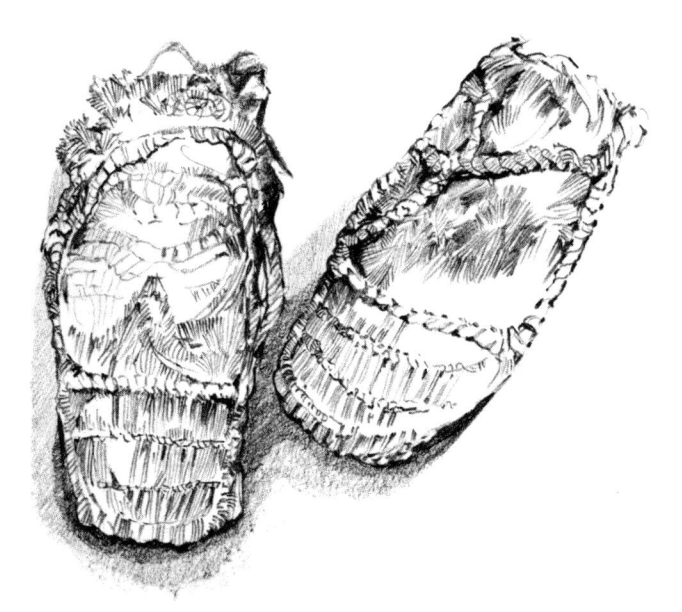

Desert people were not aimless wanderers; they possessed an intimate knowledge of their territory and its food resources at each season. Even so there were uncertainties, for rabbits were abundant one year and scarce another, while pine nuts, once gathered, were not plentiful at the same site for three or four years more.

Nothing was so important, therefore, as accurate, timely reports on the food situation in every canyon, thicket, pond, draw, and forest clearing within the radius of a few days' journey. Such information was eagerly sought when the paths of two bands or families crossed, and if they were linked by marriage, as we may suppose they usually were, then they exchanged news as friends and kinsmen. Marriage ties made it easy to assemble a large party for a collective hunt when game abounded, after which the various families might go their separate ways, each working its own cattail marsh or berry thicket. When winter came, several families would camp together, near a supply of firewood and a cache of pine nuts. Their common misery bound them to each other, because the food always gave out unless bold young hunters went into the mountains and came back with a brace of bighorn sheep.

In early spring the famished people scattered to comb the desert flats for the first clover shoots and tule stalks. If it was prickly pear country, they burned off the spines of the cactus and ate the tender pads. Later in the spring, they plucked the cactus fruit that was ripening in reddish and purplish tints along the rim of the pads. They also chewed agave leaves for the juice and spat out the fiber. Present-day archaeologists find these quids by the hundreds, along with enough human fossils to observe how the teeth were worn to the pulp by so much roughage.

A choice of foods was no part of the desert lifeway. It was the law of the desert to eat every edible plant and every crawling, swimming, flying, or running creature that could be struck with a dart or snared with a slipknot. The fleetest running creature was the pronghorn antelope, which warned its fellows of danger by raising its tail to reveal a white patch on its rump. Perhaps no man could ever have caught an antelope were it not for a stupendous drive held about once a decade in the spring, when all the band gathered. Bringing bundles of sagebrush, they constructed a corral. Then the shaman went among the animals, masked and shaking an antelope-hoof rattle. The antelopes' curiosity was their undoing, for the shaman proceeded to intrigue them and charm them into the corral, where they were dispatched at short range. It was a hugely successful stratagem, and many years passed before the antelope were again numerous enough for a drive.

Seven-year locusts, when they appeared, were driven by fire into trenches and collected, dried, and pounded into flour. There were also anthills to be taken apart for ant eggs, rodents to be roasted on a stick over a fire, chuckwallas and race-runner lizards within reach of a well-aimed stone, and minks, porcupines, and skunks, striped, spotted, and hog-nosed. Man ate them all, not scorning carnivorous bobcats and coyotes when he could get them.

After 2500 B.C. the climate improved and became much as it is today. Some of the lakes were partly restored, and after the bow and arrow reached the desert in the final centuries before Christ, it was easier to shoot waterfowl in season. But seeds, roots, and bulbs were the common mainstay of life in desert regions. In the warm months the women plied their digging sticks among the tules, gathered mesquite pods for their vile-smelling but nutritious beans, and beat the heads of wild grasses to shake out the seeds. They were racing against winter, laying aside a surplus for the bleak days ahead.

A desert-dwelling family would move about with the seasons, finding temporary quarters in a cave or erecting a conical lodge of poles, brush, and earth. They slept on grass or bark carpeting, sometimes staying long enough to misplace a bird-bone whistle or a few stone beads or California seashells. These were their little luxuries. Any woman was proud to belong to a family that owned a rabbit net, and she would scrape fiber from milkweeds and twist it into string so she might add a length to it during her lifetime. If the rabbits were plentiful in the fall, and friendly families were nearby, willing to help, her husband could be a rabbit boss and lead a drive. The net, like a tennis net but much longer, was spread in a semicircle or thrown across a draw, while men, women, and children beat the bushes for miles around and drove the frightened jackrabbits into the enclosure. There they became entangled in the meshes or were struck with throwing-clubs. Then there was feasting for many days and, best of all, there were strips of rabbit fur for sewing into robes and blankets.

Next to food, nothing was so much appreciated in wintertime as a rabbit-fur robe or a feather robe made by sewing duck skins together. The women, at least in later times, wore aprons of shredded fiber fore and aft and the men a breechclout, leggings, and sometimes a shirt.

In October or November the first frosts came to the higher wooded slopes of the Basin and the Southwest and opened the cones holding the pine nuts. This was a crucial time for the desert people. Each family, each band, had already moved to a grove that promised a good yield. Now they worked furiously, shaking the opened cones and filling their baskets with nuts which otherwise would soon fall and be lost in the forest litter. And however many they gathered, there were never enough to last through the winter. After the gathering, they decided whether to camp in the cold mountains or carry the pine nuts, a load at a time, down to a sheltered valley. But wherever the camp might be, the time came when the pine nuts were gone, and the last root and dried lily bulb had been eaten, and the people were left with their hunger and the hope of spring.

No one in the world lived closer to the ragged edge than the desert people. Diggers and seed-gatherers, they seemed of all the first Americans the least likely to succeed. Merely to stay alive, they had to untiringly exploit every resource of their desert homeland. Nothing that prowled or slithered or sprouted escaped their observation. And somewhere in the desert, it happened, there was a secret awaiting discovery by just such keen eyes.

tarch
he po
spri

8
The Great Breakthrough

M AN'S COMING TO AMERICA is an Indian story. It's not about the familiar Indians of the films and Westerns, who existed, if not exactly as in the films, some thousands of years after our story ends. The Indians we have been discussing worked out various lifeways based on combinations of hunting, fishing, and gathering wild plants. They were about as efficient as they could hope to be along those lines. The salmon fishermen of the Northwest Coast were an exception. They were on the threshold of a rich culture that would call to memory carved and painted totem poles, large plank houses, and magnificent feasts with great chieftains outdoing one another in bestowing splendid gifts. Probably no one has ever lived so well from merely appropriating the free gifts of nature.

At the other extreme were the desert people, clutching after lizards in the sun and shivering and starving in the winter. There seemed to be no way of putting aside enough food from the desert's meager offerings to last until spring. Yet the unpromising desert was to be the scene of a great breakthrough, which in the ripeness of time would enrich the lives of peoples from Canada to Chile. The breakthrough could only have occurred in favored spots under a happy combination of circumstances such as were to be found in the Valley of Tehuacán in south central Mexico.

Lying in the rain shadow of mountains that intercept the moisture-laden winds from the Gulf of Mexico, the valley receives only a modest rainfall. The caves in its cliffs are so dry that under their dusty floors a record of man's changing fortunes has been preserved from decay for 10,000 years. The litter contains fragments of whatever man ate, going back to the bones of jackrabbits and ring-tailed cats on which early hunters fed.

Though dry, this narrow valley is not all alike but changes with the seasons and varies according to altitude, slope of land, rainfall, stream flow, soil, and plant cover. In this small world, early man was not called upon, as he was in the Basin, to spend weary days trudging from sagebrush flats to pinyon pine groves. Everything was close at hand.

Plant and animal foods, though not abundant, were present in astonishing variety. Even the green iguana, a king-size lizard normally alien to these arid highlands, had somehow waded up from the wet tropics to the mesquite thickets along the lower Salado River. It made an ugly but delicious morsel. There were fish in the river, turtles in the canebrake, and opossums in the winding arroyos that carried water from the mountains, at least during the May to September rains. In that season, grass appeared on the valley floor, providing cover for cottontails. Doves and quail came to the weed patches for the ripening seeds. Lizards darted over limestone surfaces after insects. On the slopes leading to the rim of the valley were thorny acacias bearing edible pods, and prickly pear thickets, favored by wood rats, also edible.

After a summer given over to snaring game and putting away seeds, September came, with wild fruits like the chupandilla. After that the rains ceased, and the leaves fell from the desert growth or turned brown. As a result, white-tailed deer became visible and were inviting targets. Instead of huddling in bands in a winter camp, people now broke up into small hunting groups. Winters so far south are fairly mild, even in mile-high Tehuacán. But the wild ducks that came in November left in February, and by that time the deer were wary of man's wiles. So the late winter and early spring brought short rations. After the food stores were depleted, people were thankful to have a gopher or a pochote root to roast on the embers. They chewed cactus and agave tissue and wore down their teeth. Even in this favored desert region, something was missing, something that would carry man through to April when the prickly pears began ripening again on the dry slopes.

In the centuries after 6000 B.C., something *was* being tried. In the cave litter of that period, avocado seeds and chili pepper fragments appear in sizes and shapes that look less and less like wild specimens. Interesting squash seeds show up toward 5000 B.C. After that date no doubt remains that these and other plants were being cultivated by the hand of man or, more likely, woman.

The most significant of these plants is a grass bearing a few kernels, each enclosed in a separate pod. It came to be known as maize, or Indian corn, or simply corn as in the United States today. Mixed in with wild corn cultivated cobs were found, smaller than one's little toe but large in their potential. In the course of centuries, and through natural and human agencies, varieties of corn were crossed with each other and with related wild grasses until the corn acquired a sturdy stalk and bore large, many-rowed ears, sheathed in husks. Assuming various forms under man's tutelage, it spread far beyond its natural homeland, reaching New Mexico by 3500 B.C., Peru by 1500 B.C., and the eastern United States toward the beginning of the Christian era.

Though the country round and about the Valley of Tehuacán in Puebla and Oaxaca is believed to be where corn was domesticated, it was not the only hearth of agriculture. Pumpkins, first appreciated for their seeds, and bottle gourds that served as drinking vessels were cultivated in northeastern Mexico, possibly as early as 7000 B.C. Beans of many kinds were drawn into man's service in Mexico and farther south, to say nothing of potatoes in the Andes and manioc in tropical South America.

Corn, squash, and beans were the "three sisters" upon whose largesse so many of America's Indians came to subsist. They were desert born and bred, not native to the eastern woodlands or the Iowa prairies. In the Valley of Tehuacán, agriculture could start with a digging stick. There were no dense forests to clear, no tough sod to break with a plow. This high and dry region, and others like it, were relatively free of insect and fungus pests. The rain, though sparse, came in the growing season, and the streams, however intermittent their flow, did serve to moisten the bottom lands and provide water that in later centuries would be diverted into irrigated fields.

And so it came to pass that the last were first and that from the seed-gathering desert people came the inventors of New World agriculture. On second thought, it is not so surprising that gatherers of seeds should hit upon the secret of planting them, especially in favored spots like Tehuacán, where plants of many kinds were close at hand and people seldom wandered too far away to keep an eye on a garden or look in on a patch of sown grass.

Nothing since man had reached the human state was to have such far-reaching consequences as the great breakthrough that transformed him from a food gatherer into a food producer. The change came about almost imperceptibly, perhaps beginning with such half measures as were later observed in the Great Basin: burning a field to encourage a better wild tobacco crop, digging a channel to draw melting snow to the pigweed, or scattering wild grass seed on soil prepared for it.

That seeds would sprout was surely well known to people who spent much time observing them. The secret lay in fitting new chores like clearing, planting, cultivating, weeding, and harvesting into an old lifeway. At first, in the view of prejudiced male hunters, it must have seemed hardly worth the trouble except as something women could do while minding the children. At a time not long before 5000 B.C., only five percent of the food consumed at Tehuacán came from cultivated plants. A primitive ear of corn was a snack that one chewed, husk and all, for the sweetness, then spat out the quid. Not till 3,000 years later did the ear show promise of becoming the staff of life. By then a third of the diet was derived from corn and other cultivated foods, the rest from wild plants and game. But the trend to agriculture was running strong, and the farmers' clustered huts were beginning to look like permanent villages. The story of what lay ahead may be deciphered at higher levels of the excavated sites, which reveal the growth of towns and temple centers and close relations with rising civilizations elsewhere in Mexico.

Not long ago, agriculture was regarded as something too extraordinary to have been invented more than once. It was seen as stemming from the Near East, where wheat and barley, along with sheep and goats, were evidently domesticated between 9000 and 7000 B.C. That other peoples, and least of all the far removed Indians, should follow a parallel course was regarded as unthinkable. But now we know that agriculture is nearly as old in Mexico as in Southwest Asia. It dates from times before there were ships capable of crossing oceans or anyone except nonfarming hunters was crossing the Bering Strait.

The present view is that various Old and New World peoples, working separately on familiar plants and animals, share the honors of inventing agriculture. And why shouldn't they have done so, being of the same *Homo sapiens sapiens* stock, having the same human potential? After our world pulled out of the Ice Age, the lifeways of the woodland hunters of western Europe and of the eastern United States were surprisingly alike. Wild foods were available in great variety, but it was in more arid, less wooded lands that the wild ancestors of the basic Old and New World cereals were waiting to be domesticated. The arts of cultivation spread slowly into the forests of Europe and North America, where plots had to be cleared with stone axes, and did not reach England until near 3000 B.C. This was some three thousand years after the beginnings of farming in Mexico. But we should not assume that the people then inhabiting England were less clever than the Mexican Indians. They were just technologically underdeveloped for the time and terrain in which they lived.

Now a word about any latecomers who may have reached America by crossing the wide Pacific. We have noted the curious pottery that appears on the Ecuador coast about 3200 B.C., inspired, some believe, by Japanese fishermen who were blown off their course and cast up on these shores. We might add the mystery of cotton, since it was domesticated, spun, and woven quite early in Mexico and Peru and seems to be a cross between Old World and New World species. Can it be accounted for without supposing that somebody brought the seeds of one of its ancestors across the ocean thousands of years ago? That is a question that divides the experts. For that matter, everything that touches on trans-Pacific contacts seems to be controversial.

Distinguished scholars may be found on both sides of this question, which spills over beyond the time of our story; it is mentioned here because it has to do with men who may have reached America before the Europeans did.

Those belonging to one school of thought believe that the high cultures of Mexico and the Andes owe much of their splendor to ideas that diffused from Asia after about 700 B.C., when Chinese mariners became capable of long sea voyages. In the jaguar cult that flourished in these areas these scholars see the influence of the Chinese tiger. The oriental dragon lives on, they say, in the scroll patterns of Mexican sculpture. Jade carving, a difficult art, was practiced on both sides of the Pacific, while three-legged pottery jars were shaped alike, even to a little bird that sits on the lid. In the early centuries of the Christian era, designs popular in India and Southeast Asia have striking counterparts in Mayan art, such as flowering lotus plants, tiger thrones, sea monsters, and the tree of life. Also shared by Asia and America are the panpipe, a wind instrument, and miniature copper axes that did duty for money.

Those in the other school hold that, just as the American Indians came independently to agriculture, so they created their own high cultures with little or no help from across the Pacific. They see American art styles, jade carving, temple centers, and a calendar system all well under way before the supposed Chinese sea voyages. Why, they ask, should Asian seafarers come with pottery bowls and lotus designs and neglect to bring rice and pigs? Similar designs do not prove contact, they contend. It is the resemblances that get noticed, while the differences are ignored. The pyramids of Egypt have no likely connection with those of Mexico. A Greek coin of the fifth century before Christ shows an eagle perched on a stone and grappling with a serpent. The same theme figures in Aztec religious art, but is surely not inspired from Greece. There remains the mystery of the sweet potato, found in both Polynesia and Peru and bearing a similar name. It seems more likely to have been carried from South America to the islands than the other way around. Polynesian influences, if any, were late and could only have arrived after Peru was already on the high road to civilization.

So runs the debate, an important one, because ancient America is a sort of laboratory in which it may be possible to find out whether peoples who are separated from one another are unlikely to hit upon the same idea, if it is very complicated, or whether, in similar circumstances, they are apt to find similar solutions for their problems. The more American man is found to have been isolated since early hunting days, the more credit he deserves for independent inventions. Perhaps only young readers will live to know how the debate turns out. At present, a nose count of the experts seems to show a few with strong opinions one way or the other and a majority who regard occasional trans-Pacific contacts as quite possible but tend to minimize their influence, rating it from moderate to almost nil.

One thing is sure. No domesticated animals were brought from the Old World to the New, unless it was the dog by way of the Bering Strait. The Indians knew the wild animals around them well and would return from the hunt with bear cubs and fledgling eagles for the amusement and education of their children. But the creatures that remained docile when grown were few. The cow had not made it to America; the horse was extinct. The buffalo might seem a promising candidate for domesticity — George Washington once thought so — but it has consistently declined to work for man. Dogs were harnessed to the sled in the Arctic and to the travois on the Plains. Llamas and alpacas carried small loads in the Andes at a reluctant pace. After that, the list of creatures disposed to live with man trails off to guinea pigs, turkeys, ducks, and bees.

It is no reflection on man in America that, lacking suitable livestock, he failed to drink milk, ride on an animal's back, and build wagons and war chariots. Wheels he found useful only to put on his children's toys. Though a hunter and meat-eater by background, he came to live in communities that soon outgrew the supply of game. Thus he strove to make up in plants what he lacked in animals. Beans of many kinds supplied him with proteins, and he went on to domesticate and improve peanuts, pineapples, tomatoes, papayas, vanilla, cacao for chocolate, and well over a hundred other useful plants, including trees yielding rubber, chicle for chewing gum, and bark for quinine. Today these Indian gifts supply the world with nearly half its food of vegetable origin. Though the Old World has twice the land area of the New, Indian corn and potatoes rank along with rice and wheat as the world's four major crops.

Poor in docile animals, the New World also lacked a Mediterranean, a sea in the middle of the land that would make for easy sailing between the peoples. There were lake and river craft, as well as large merchant canoes engaged in coastwide trade along the Gulf of Mexico and in the Caribbean. Columbus came upon one such canoe off the Honduras coast, with a crew of twenty-five and a cargo of clothing and copper bells. But these water routes did not link the centers of high culture, which were strung out in the highlands and forests on America's long north-and-south axis. An Aztec chronicle relates that traveling merchants were obliged to climb up and down mountains and canyons "on elbow and knee." With communications so difficult, the flow of stimulating ideas between one rising civilization and another was impeded.

Nevertheless, the notion that Indian culture was stagnating until nudged by the Europeans has been exploded. Radiocarbon dates now mark the stages by which man, after coming to America, made subtle adjustments to the most varied environments. They show him experimenting with weeds and grasses and multiplying the size of their edible parts. They pinpoint the spread of his plants far beyond their original habitats: we know, for example, that corn reached the present site of Kansas City about the time of Christ. And we know that in the thousand years or so before and after that time, Indian lifeways were undergoing an astonishing transformation.

This was the time when metallurgy was spreading from the Andes into Central America and Mexico and exquisite jewels were cast in gold, silver, and alloys. Before A.D. 1000 the secret of bronze, a copper-tin alloy, was known in South America. Would iron have remained forever a mystery?

Consider only a few highlights. Textiles of a weave too fine to be equaled today were made in Peru. In Mexico, characters were carved on stone and painted on paper, beginning as pictures and coming to represent ideas and even sounds, thus repeating the stages by which writing developed in the Old World. No one anywhere knew the length of the year as accurately as the Mayas. Arithmetic was far easier for them than for the Romans, since in the Maya system a number's value depended on its position and every empty space carried a zero sign. By A.D. 300, Teotihuacán, in the Valley of

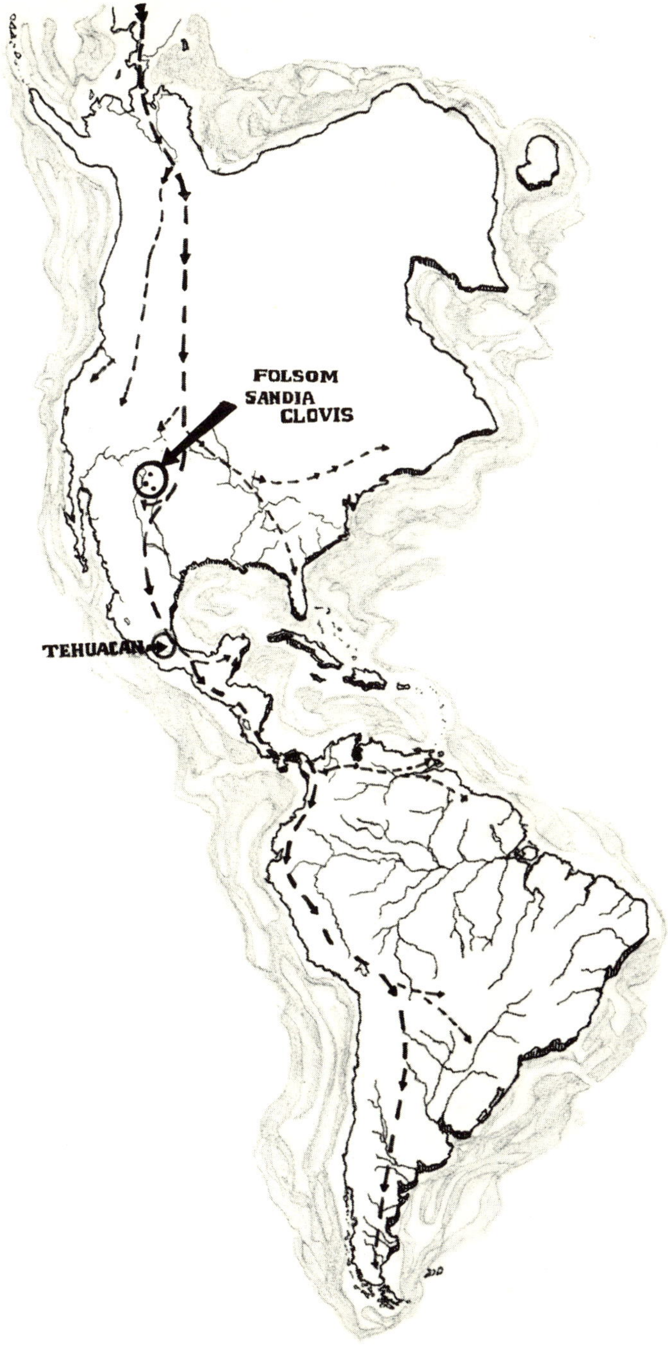
FOLSOM
SANDIA
CLOVIS
TEHUACAN

Mexico, had not only its sun and moon pyramids but a population of perhaps 100,000, and was one of the world's largest cities, a busy center of crafts and trade. Soon Mexican influences were making over lifeways in the United States, as manifest by the extensive irrigation works of the Southwest, the temple mounds grouped around plazas on the Mississippi and its tributaries, and the well-ordered towns to which the people of the Southeast, after working together in the cornfields, came for dancing and ball games.

Thus, in the centuries before the Europeans came, man the hunter and seed-gatherer was becoming man the farmer, craftsman, priest, merchant, chieftain, and even king. He was man the warrior, too, eager for glory. Sometimes he did his prisoners the honor of torturing them so they might demonstrate their courage. Sometimes he adopted them into his family or band. If he made war, he also smoked the calumet, buried the hatchet, and sealed treaties with gifts of wampum. To preserve the peace with his neighbors, he organized the League of the Iroquois in New York State and the Confederation of Anáhuac in the Valley of Mexico. He treated children tenderly, and all his life enjoyed the emotional security of belonging to a close-knit group. When experience had not made him wary, he was courteous and hospitable to strangers. Often he was a poet, and many of his sensitive reflections on beauty, friendship, and the brevity of life have survived and been written down in Mexico.

Man was also a shaman, sometimes his own, as when he went on a vision quest on the Plains, fasting in retreat until a guardian spirit came to aid and counsel him. He had various names for a spiritual force that seemed to him to permeate all things, and he felt himself to be a part of nature, rather than to stand outside it. In the higher cultures, the priest overshadowed the shaman, and man made offerings to gods of the sun, rain, and corn. For many, these and other deities came to represent aspects of the Giver of Life, so often mentioned in Aztec literature, a force at once male and female, existing beyond time and space, invisible like night, impalpable like the wind, but ever present in their hearts.

Early man in America was different from man in the Old World — yet perhaps not so different. He was part of the great dispersal that carried the human race to every habitable part of the world. He was a pioneer. No one else had traveled so far. Coming to America, its true discoverer, he transformed an entire hemisphere into a home for mankind.

Further Reading

Those who would like to know more about the materials discussed in the preceding pages will find the following books and articles helpful. They range from popular to scholarly in style. Highly specialized technical papers are not included except for a very few that are indispensable for clarifying major problems. Several of the references listed below, including the college texts, carry extensive bibliographies dealing with individual sites, tool and weapon types, and archaeological theory.

New developments come thick and fast and are reported, among other places, in *American Antiquity, American Anthropologist, Science, Scientific American,* state and regional archaeological journals, and monographs published by foundations, museums, and university presses.

GENERAL WORKS

PREHISTORY

Bordes, François. *The Old Stone Age.* McGraw-Hill, New York, 1968.
    Main lines of development throughout the world.

Braidwood, Robert J., and Gordon R. Willey, eds. *Courses Toward Urban Life.* Aldine, Chicago, 1962. Symposium on man from late Ice Age times to the threshold of urban civilizations, including five papers on American regions.

Caldwell, Joseph R., ed. *New Roads to Yesterday.* Basic Books, New York, 1966. Selections from *Science.*
Chard, Chester S. *Man in Prehistory.* McGraw-Hill, New York, 1969. From the achievement of humanity to the threshold of civilization. A college text.
Clark, Grahame. *World Prehistory: A New Outline.* Cambridge University Press, New York, 2d edition, 1969.
Clark, Grahame, and Stuart Piggott. *Prehistoric Societies.* Knopf, New York, 1965.
Howell, F. Clark, and the editors of Time-Life Books. *Early Man.* Life Nature Library, Time-Life Books, New York, 1965. Richly illustrated, highly readable.
Howells, William. *Mankind in the Making: The Story of Human Evolution.* Doubleday, Garden City, N.Y., revised edition, 1967.
Lee, Richard B., and Irven DeVore, eds. *Man the Hunter.* Aldine, Chicago, 1968. A symposium on hunting and gathering peoples of the world.
Montagu, Ashley. *Man: His First Two Million Years.* Columbia University Press, New York, 1969.
Oakley, Kenneth P. *Man the Tool-Maker.* Trustees of the British Museum, London, 5th edition, 1961.
Service, Elman R. *The Hunters.* Prentice-Hall, Englewood Cliffs, N.J., 1966.
Tax, Sol, ed. *Horizons of Anthropology.* Aldine, Chicago, 1964. Broadcast lectures on what we know and what we have yet to learn about human nature and behavior.
Trustees of the British Museum. *Flint Implements: An Account of Stone Age Techniques and Cultures.* London, 3rd edition, 1968.

AMERICAN INDIANS

Brennan, Louis A. *American Dawn: A New Model of American Prehistory.* Macmillan, New York, 1970.
Bryan, Alan Lyle. *Paleo-American Prehistory.* Occasional Papers of the Idaho State University Museum, No. 16, Pocatello, Idaho, 1965.
Driver, Harold E. *Indians of North America.* University of Chicago Press, Chicago, 2d edition revised, 1969. Chiefly on culture in historical times. Chapter 1 treats "Origin and Prehistory."
Farb, Peter. *Man's Rise to Civilization as Shown by the Indians of North America from Primeval Times to the Coming of the Industrial State.* Dutton, New York, 1968.
Hibben, Frank C. *Digging Up America.* Hill and Wang, New York, 1960.
Jennings, Jesse D. *Prehistory of North America.* McGraw-Hill, New York, 1968. Area culture histories from the peopling of the New World. A college text.
Jennings, Jesse D., and Edward Norbeck, eds. *Prehistoric Man in the New World.* University of Chicago Press, Chicago, 1964. Specialists summarize what is known, area by area.

FURTHER READING 141

Josephy, Alvin M., Jr. *The Indian Heritage of America*. Knopf, New York, 1968.
Macgowan, Kenneth, and Joseph A. Hester, Jr. *Early Man in the New World*. Natural History Library, Garden City, N.Y., 1962.
Sanders, William T., and Joseph Marino. *New World Prehistory*. Prentice-Hall, Englewood Cliffs, N.J., 1970.
Spencer, Robert F., Jesse D. Jennings, and others. *The Native Americans: Prehistory and Ethnology of the North American Indians*. Harper, New York, 1965.
Willey, Gordon R. *An Introduction to American Archaeology*. Vol. I, *North and Middle America*. Prentice-Hall, Englewood Cliffs, N.J., 1966. A richly illustrated summary for students and general readers.
Willey, Gordon R., ed. *Prehistoric Settlement Patterns in the New World*. Viking Fund Publications in Anthropology, New York, 1956.
Wormington, H. M. *Ancient Man in North America*. Denver Museum of Natural History, Denver, Colo., 4th edition, 1957. Many descriptions of early man sites.

ARCHAEOLOGY, ANTHROPOLOGY, AND RELATED FIELDS

Braidwood, Robert J. *Archeologists and What They Do*. Franklin Watts, New York, 1960. A professional describes his field for young readers.
Brothwell, Don, and Eric Higgs, eds. *Science in Archaeology*. Praeger, New York, revised edition, 1970. Fifty-four reports on methods employed to gain a better understanding of man's past.
Brown, Ina Corinne. *Understanding Other Cultures*. Prentice-Hall, Englewood Cliffs, N.J., 1963. An introduction to anthropology for young readers.
Cahalane, Victor H. *Mammals of North America*. Macmillan, New York, 1966.
Daniel, Glyn. *Origins and Growth of Archaeology*. Penguin, Baltimore, 1970.
Deetz, James. *Invitation to Archaeology*. Natural History Press, Garden City, N.Y., 1967.
Edel, May. *The Story of People: Anthropology for Young People*. Little, Brown, Boston, 1953.
Flannery, Kent V. "Culture History v. Cultural Process: A Debate in American Archaeology." *Scientific American* 217:2 (Aug. 1967), pp. 119–122. Two approaches to archaeology compared.
Gorenstein, Shirley. *Introduction to Archaeology*. Basic Books, New York, 1965.
Heizer, Robert F., ed. *The Archaeologist at Work: A Source Book in Archaeological Method and Interpretation*. Harper, New York, 1959.
Hole, Frank, and Robert F. Heizer. *Introduction to Prehistoric Archaeology*. Holt, New York, 2d edition, 1969. How archaeologists go about their work.
Knight, Clifford B. *Basic Concepts of Ecology*. Macmillan, New York, 1965.

Mead, Margaret. *Anthropologists and What They Do.* Franklin Watts, New York, 1965. An informative account for young adults.
Piggott, Stuart, ed. *Approach to Archaeology.* McGraw-Hill, New York, 1965.
Wheeler, Mortimer. *Archaeology from the Earth.* Penguin, Baltimore, 1956.
Willey, Gordon R., and Philip Phillips. *Method and Theory in American Archaeology.* University of Chicago Press, Chicago, 1958.

CHAPTER REFERENCES
(Titles listed above under "General Works" are carried here by author's name only.)

1: LIKE NO OTHER ANIMAL

Campbell, Bernard G. *Human Evolution: An Introduction to Man's Adaptations.* Aldine, Chicago, 1966. See especially "Reproduction, the Family, and Social Structure," pp. 246–285; "Culture and Society," pp. 286–325; "The Origin of Man," pp. 326–366.
Clark, J. Desmond. "The Evolution of Culture in Africa." *The American Naturalist,* 97:892 (Jan.–Feb. 1963), pp. 15–28. (Also as Social Sciences Reprint No. A-281, Bobbs-Merrill, Indianapolis, Ind.)
Cohen, Yehudi A., ed. *Man in Adaptation: The Biosocial Background.* Aldine, Chicago, 1968. How man emerged and evolved: selected readings.
———. *Man in Adaptation: The Cultural Present.* Aldine, Chicago, 1968. See especially pp. 7–60 for significance of culture.
Coles, J. M., and E. S. Higgs. *The Archaeology of Early Man.* Praeger, New York, 1969. See "Chronology, Ecology and Economy," pp. 25–75.
Dobzhansky, Theodosius. *Mankind Evolving: The Evolution of the Human Species.* Yale University Press, New Haven, Conn., 1962. Culture, heredity, and man's emergence — a solid book for advanced readers.
Eimerl, Sarel, Irven DeVore, and the editors of *Life. The Primates.* Life Nature Library, Time, Inc., New York, 1965. Up-to-date, well-illustrated report on man's nearest relatives.
Eiseley, Loren. *The Firmament of Time.* Atheneum, New York, 1960. Discusses geology, evolution, and the Ice Age. See especially Chapter 4, "How Man Became Natural."
Howell, F. Clark. "The Villafranchian and Human Origins." In Caldwell, pp. 33–77. (Also in *Science* 130:831–844, Oct. 2, 1959.)
Hulse, Frederick S. *The Human Species.* Random House, New York, 1963.
Leakey, L. S. B., and Vanne Morris Goodall. *Unveiling Man's Origins.* Schenkman, Cambridge, Mass., 1968. Man's discovery of his own past.
Oakley, Kenneth. *Frameworks for Dating Fossil Man.* Aldine, Chicago, 2d edition, 1966. A technical work. Fossil hominid dating tables on pp. 296–341.
Underhill, Ruth M. *First Came the Family.* Morrow, New York, 1958. For young readers.

FURTHER READING

Washburn, Sherwood L., ed. *Social Life of Early Man.* Aldine, Chicago, 1961. Selected readings stemming from a conference on the group behavior of primates and man.
See also Bordes, pp. 9–97; Chard, pp. 58–115; Clark, pp. 5–42; Clark and Piggott, pp. 27–54; Howell, pp. 9–121; Howells, pp. 15–188; Oakley, pp. 1–54; Tax, pp. 15–119; Trustees of the British Museum, pp. 9–58.

2: COMING TO TERMS WITH THE COLD

Butzer, Karl W. *Environment and Archeology: An Introduction to Pleistocene Geography.* Aldine, Chicago, 1964. See pp. 252–257 for Ice Age animals; pp. 373–383 for Neanderthal Man and the Lebenstedt site; pp. 384–395 for blade-tool makers and cold-climate clothing and settlement patterns.
Klíma, Bohuslav. "The First Ground-Plan of an Upper Paleolithic Loess Settlement in Middle Europe and Its Meaning." In Braidwood and Willey, pp. 193–210. The Dolni Vestonice site.
Leroi-Gourhan, André. "The Evolution of Paleolithic Art." *Scientific American* 218:2 (Feb. 1968), pp. 58–70.
Okladnikov, A. P. "The Temperate Zone of Continental Asia." In Braidwood and Willey, pp. 267–287. Malta and other Siberian sites. Later excavations at Malta are described by M. M. Gerasimov in Michael, Henry N., ed., *The Archaeology and Geomorphology of Northern Asia,* University of Toronto Press, Toronto, 1964, pp. 3–32. See also Clark, pp. 62–64.
See also Bordes, pp. 98–212; Chard, pp. 115–169; Clark, pp. 42–69; Clark and Piggott, pp. 55–101; Howell, pp. 122–191; Howells, pp. 189–247; Oakley, pp. 54–88; Trustees of the British Museum, pp. 58–69.

3: WHO CAME AND WHEN?

Campbell, Joseph. *The Masks of God: Primitive Mythology.* Viking, New York, 1959. "The Mythology of the Primitive Hunters," pp. 229–354, discusses shamanism, the animal master, and bear cults.
Chang, Kwang-chih. *The Archaeology of Ancient China.* Yale University Press, New Haven, Conn., revised edition, 1968. See especially "Palaeolithic and Mesolithic Foundations," pp. 39–77.
Eiseley, Loren C. "The Paleo-Indians: Their Survival and Diffusion." In *New Interpretations of Aboriginal American Culture History,* Anthropological Society of Washington, 1955, pp. 1–11. (Also as Social Sciences Reprint No. A-58, Bobbs-Merrill, Indianapolis, Ind.) Man follows the grass-eating animals into the New World: a classic piece.
Eliade, Mircea. *Shamanism: Archaic Techniques of Ecstasy.* Princeton University Press, Princeton, N.J., 1964.
Giddings, J. L. "The Archeology of Bering Strait." *Current Anthropology* 1:2 (March 1960), pp. 121–138. (Also as Social Sciences Reprint No. A-297, Bobbs-Merrill, Indianapolis, Ind.) The area as a culture center, with comments by other archaeologists.
Griffin, James B. "Some Prehistoric Connections between Siberia and

America." In Caldwell, pp. 277-301. (Also in *Science* 131:801-812, March 18, 1960.)
Gruhn, Ruth. "Two Early Radiocarbon Dates from the Lower Levels of Wilson Butte Cave, South Central Idaho." *Tebiwa*, Idaho State University Museum, Pocatello, Idaho, 8:2 (1965), p. 57.
Hopkins, David M. "The Cenozoic History of Beringia — A Synthesis." In Hopkins, David M., ed., *The Bering Land Bridge*, Stanford University Press, Stanford, Calif., 1967, pp. 451-484. Summing up a symposium on the land bridge.
Krieger, Alex D. "Early Man in the New World." In Jennings and Norbeck, pp. 23-81. Includes the case for preprojectile-point stage. For a contrary view, on geological grounds, see Haynes, C. Vance, Jr., "Fluted Projectile Points: Their Age and Dispersion," *Science* 145: 1408-1413, Sept. 25, 1964. See also Brennan, pp. 119-151; Jennings, pp. 65-70; Spencer and Jennings, p. 20; Willey, pp. 29-37, 454-457.
Lanning, Edward P., and Thomas C. Patterson. "Early Man in South America." *Scientific American* 217:5 (Nov. 1967), pp. 44-50.
Laughlin, W. S. "Human Migration and Permanent Occupation in the Bering Sea Area." In Hopkins, David M., ed., *The Bering Land Bridge*, Stanford University Press, Stanford, Calif., 1967, pp. 409-450.
Leakey, L. S. B., and others. "Archaeological Excavations in the Calico Mountains, California: Preliminary Report." *Science* 160:1022-1023, May 31, 1968. The controversial Mohave Desert site.
Lynch, Thomas F., and Kenneth A. R. Kennedy. "Early Human Cultural and Skeletal Remains from Guitarrero Cave, Northern Peru." *Science* 169:1307-1309, Sept. 27, 1970. A radiocarbon date of 10,610 B.C.
MacNeish, Richard S. "Early Man in the Andes." *Scientific American* 224:4 (Apr. 1971), pp. 36-46. Finds in Peru indicating that "we must push back the date of man's earliest appearance in South America . . . to perhaps as much as 20,000 B.C."
Maringer, Johannes. *The Gods of Prehistoric Man.* Knopf, New York, 1960. See pp. 3-160 for hunting rites, burial practices, emergence of art, the bear cult, and "mother goddesses."
Müller-Beck, Hansjürgen. "On Migrations of Hunters Across the Bering Land Bridge in the Upper Pleistocene." In Hopkins, David M., ed., *The Bering Land Bridge*, Stanford University Press, Stanford, Calif., 1967, pp. 373-408. Müller-Beck's case for migrations from Siberia as early as 28,000 years ago is also presented in *Science* 152:1191-1210, May 27, 1966.
Norbeck, Edward. *Religion in Primitive Society.* Harper, New York, 1961.
Okladnikov, A. P. "The Petroglyphs of Siberia." *Scientific American* 221:2 (Aug. 1969), pp. 74-82.
Radin, Paul. *The Trickster: A Study in American Indian Mythology.* Greenwood, New York, 1969.
Swadesh, Morris. "Linguistic Overview." In Jennings and Norbeck, pp. 527-556. The movement of languages into the New World. On Indian

languages, see also Driver, pp. 25-52; Josephy, pp. 12-22; Spencer and Jennings, pp. 100-118; Willey, pp. 16-19.

Thompson, Stith. *Tales of the North American Indians*. Indiana University Press, Bloomington, 1966.

Underhill, Ruth M. *Red Man's Religion*. University of Chicago Press, Chicago, 1965. A fascinating account by a first-hand observer.

Wauchope, Robert. *Lost Tribes and Sunken Continents: Myth and Method in the Study of American Indians*. University of Chicago Press, Chicago, 1962.

For the discovery of Folsom points, see Macgowan and Hester, pp. 144-154; Wormington, pp. 23-42. For possible influences from China and elsewhere in East Asia, see Chard, pp. 113, 120, 141-147; Howells, pp. 306-309; Willey, pp. 33-37. Physical traits of early Americans are discussed in Howells, pp. 293-306; Jennings, pp. 45-53; Macgowan and Hester, pp. 119-142, 207-231; Spencer and Jennings, pp. 20-23; Willey, pp. 12-16. For house types, see Driver, pp. 116-135.

4: THE HEYDAY OF HUNTING

Bennett, Wendell C., and Junius B. Bird. *Andean Culture History*. Natural History Press, Garden City, N.Y., 2d and revised edition, 1960.

Birdsell, Joseph B. "Some Predictions for the Pleistocene Based on Equilibrium Systems among Recent Hunter-Gatherers." In Lee and DeVore, pp. 229-249. On the size of hunting bands. See also papers by B. J. Williams, pp. 126-131, and Julian H. Steward, pp. 321-334.

Borden, Charles E. "New Evidence on the Early Peopling of the New World." In *Britannica Book of the Year, 1969*, Encyclopaedia Britannica, Chicago, pp. 101-103. Possible population movements south from Alaska with microblade technology as Ice Age ended.

Bushnell, G. H. S. *Peru*. Praeger, New York, 1957. See especially pp. 13-34.

Haury, Emil W., E. B. Sayles, and William W. Wasley. "The Lehner Mammoth Site, Southeastern Arizona." *American Antiquity* 25:1 (July 1959), pp. 2-30. (Also as Social Sciences Reprint No. A-305, Bobbs-Merrill, Indianapolis, Ind.)

Haynes, C. Vance, Jr. "Elephant-hunting in North America." *Scientific American* 214:6 (June 1966), pp. 104-112.

Lanning, Edward P. *Peru before the Incas*. Prentice-Hall, Englewood Cliffs, N.J., 1967. See especially pp. 1-56.

Reichel-Dolmatoff, G. *Colombia*. Praeger, New York, 1965. See especially pp. 17-60.

Wedel, Waldo R. "The Great Plains." In Jennings and Norbeck, pp. 193-220.

Wendorf, Fred, and James J. Hester. "Early Man's Utilization of the Great Plains Environment." *American Antiquity* 28:2 (Autumn 1962), pp. 159-171. (Also as Social Sciences Reprint No. A-360, Bobbs-Merrill, Indianapolis, Ind.)

Wheat, Joe Ben. "A Paleo-Indian Bison Kill." *Scientific American* 216:1

(Jan. 1967), pp. 44-52. How hunters stampeded a herd in Colorado 10,000 years ago.
See also Bordes, pp. 213-219; Brennan, pp. 78-87; Clark, pp. 269-276; Jennings, pp. 71-108; Josephy, pp. 37-48; Macgowan and Hester, pp. 11-28, 154-205; Spencer and Jennings, pp. 23-39; Willey, pp. 37-55, 64-68, 72-73, 457-458; Wormington, pp. 250-251. In a section on forms of kinship, Service, pp. 32-42, discusses the whys of marriage.

5: FOREST AND SHORE

Coe, Michael D. *Mexico.* Praeger, New York, 1967. See especially Chapter 2, "Early Hunters," and Chapter 3, "The Archaic Period."
Coe, Michael D., and Kent V. Flannery. "Microenvironments and Mesoamerican History." In Caldwell, pp. 348-359. (Also in *Science* 143:650-655, Feb. 14, 1964.)
Covarrubias, Miguel. *The Eagle, the Jaguar, and the Serpent: Indian Art of the Americas. North America: Alaska, Canada, the United States.* Knopf, New York, 1954. Also *Indian Art of Mexico and Central America,* 1957.
Evans, Clifford. "Lowland South America." In Jennings and Norbeck, pp. 419-450.
Gilmore, Raymond M. "Fauna and Ethnozoology of South America." In *Handbook of South American Indians,* vol. 6, Smithsonian Institution, Washington, D.C., 1950, pp. 345-467. A technical paper on animals available to early hunters, interspersed with many facts of popular interest.
Griffin, James B. "Eastern North American Archaeology: A Summary." Science 156:175-191, Apr. 14, 1967.
———. "The Northeast Woodlands Area." In Jennings and Norbeck, pp. 223-258.
Heizer, Robert F. "Primitive Man as an Ecologic Factor." *Kroeber Anthropological Society Papers,* No. 13, 1955, pp. 1-31. (Also as Social Sciences Reprint No. A-366, Bobbs-Merrill, Indianapolis, Ind.) Conservation practices of American Indians and others.
———. "The Western Coast of North America." In Jennings and Norbeck, pp. 117-148.
Holmberg, Allan R. *Nomads of the Long Bow: The Siriono of Eastern Bolivia.* Natural History Press, Garden City, N.Y., 1969. An anthropologist reports on a living Old Stone Age tropical forest people.
Laughlin, William S. "Hunting: An Integrating Biobehavior System and Its Evolutionary Importance." In Lee and DeVore, pp. 304-320. "Programming children" for their life work. See also Driver, pp. 97-98.
Lowie, Robert H. "The Tropical Forests: An Introduction." *Handbook of South American Indians,* vol. 3. Smithsonian Institution, Washington, D.C., 1948, pp. 1-56.
Meggers, Betty J. *Ecuador.* Praeger, New York, 1966. See especially pp. 16-54.

Meggers, Betty J., and Clifford Evans. "A Transpacific Contact in 3000 B.C." *Scientific American* 214:1 (Jan. 1966), pp. 28-35. The case for the Japanese inspiration of an early pottery type in Ecuador. For a dissenting view, see Lathrap, Donald, in *American Anthropologist* 69:1 (Feb. 1967), pp. 96-98.

Quimby, George Irving. *Indian Life in the Upper Great Lakes, 11,000 B.C to A.D. 1800.* University of Chicago Press, Chicago, 1960. For general readers and beginning students. See especially "The Changing World of the Old Copper Indians," pp. 52-63.

Rouse, Irving. "The Caribbean Area." In Jennings and Norbeck, pp. 389-417.

——. "Prehistory of the West Indies." In Caldwell, pp. 380-410. (Also in *Science* 144:499-513, May 1, 1964.)

Sears, William H. "The Southeastern United States." In Jennings and Norbeck, pp. 259-287.

Spaulding, Albert C. "Prehistoric Cultural Development in the Eastern United States." In *New Interpretations of Aboriginal American Culture History*, Anthropological Society of Washington, D.C., 1955, pp. 12-27. (Also as Social Sciences Reprints No. A-209, Bobbs-Merrill, Indianapolis, Ind.)

Steward, Julian H., and Louis C. Faron. *Native Peoples of South America.* McGraw-Hill, New York, 1959.

For the Archaic stage, see Jennings, pp. 109-134; Spencer and Jennings, pp. 39-40, 47-56; Willey, pp. 60-64, 246-266, 311-317, 370-374, 380-394, 396-404, 458-459, 464-467, 477. The conventional view that the Archaic developed out of the big-game hunting tradition is challenged in various passages by Bryan and Brennan. For life at the tip of South America, see Campbell, Joseph, *The Masks of God: Primitive Mythology*, Viking, New York, 1959, pp. 245-251, 315-322; also Jennings, p. 79; Montagu, pp. 143-144, 147; Service, p. 75. Salmon fishing and associated beliefs in the Pacific Northwest are described in Spencer and Jennings, pp. 175-177, 200; California lifeways in Driver, p. 91; Sanders and Marino, pp. 31-32; Willey, pp. 361-374. For peacekeeping and absence of sustained warfare, see Service, pp. 55-61.

6: ESKIMO LIFEWAYS

Anderson, Douglas D. "A Stone Age Campsite at the Gateway to America." *Scientific American* 218:6 (June 1968), pp. 24-33.

Balikci, Asen. "The Netsilik Eskimos: Adaptive Processes." In Lee and DeVore, pp. 78-82. Annual hunting rounds in the central Arctic.

Collins, Henry B. "The Arctic and Subarctic." In Jennings and Norbeck, pp. 85-114.

Early Man in the Western American Arctic. A Symposium. Anthropological Papers of the University of Alaska, College, Alaska, 10:2 (Apr. 1963). Contributions by J. L. Giddings, Henry B. Collins, Hans-Georg Bandi, John M. Campbell, Frederick Hadleigh West, William N.

Irving, W. S. Laughlin, Richard S. MacNeish, H. M. Wormington, Chester S. Chard.

Freuchen, Peter. *Book of the Eskimos*. World, Cleveland, 1961. Personal, highly readable account of life in the Arctic.

Giddings, J. Louis. *Ancient Man of the Arctic*. Knopf, New York, 1967. An archaeologist's personal account. Exciting, humorous, informative.

Laughlin, William S. "Eskimos and Aleuts: Their Origins and Evolution." In Caldwell, pp. 247–276. (Also in *Science* 142:633–645, Nov. 8, 1963.)

Laughlin, W. S. "Human Migration and Permanent Occupation in the Bering Sea Area." In Hopkins, David M., ed., *The Bering Land Bridge*, Stanford University Press, Stanford, Calif., 1967, pp. 409–450. Includes report on Anangula.

Versions of the Sedna story appear in Freuchen (above), pp. 234–235, and Thompson, Stith, *Tales of North American Indians*, Indiana University Press, Bloomington, 1966, pp. 3–4. Other Eskimo references: Farb, pp. 34–66; Jennings, pp. 287–320; Josephy, pp. 57–72; Spencer and Jennings, pp. 119–167; Willey, pp. 69–72, 410–453.

7: THE DESERT PEOPLE

Jennings, Jesse D. "The Desert West." In Jennings and Norbeck, pp. 149–174.

Reed, Erik K. "The Greater Southwest." In Jennings and Norbeck, pp. 175–191.

Steward, Julian H. "The Great Basin Shoshonean Indians: An Example of a Family Level of Sociocultural Integration." In Cohen, Yehudi A., ed., *Man in Adaptation: The Cultural Present*, Aldine, Chicago, 1968, pp. 68–81.

See also Farb, pp. 16–33; Jennings, pp. 134–163; Spencer and Jennings, pp. 39–42, 264–285; Willey, pp. 55–60, 178–186, 342–361.

8: THE GREAT BREAKTHROUGH

Adams, Robert McC. *The Evolution of Urban Society: Early Mesopotamia and Prehispanic Mexico*. Aldine, Chicago, 1966.

Armillas, Pedro. "Northern Mesoamerica." In Jennings and Norbeck, pp. 291–329.

Byers, Douglas S., ed. *The Prehistory of the Tehuacan Valley*, vol. 1, *Environment and Subsistence*. University of Texas Press, Austin, 1967. Experts in various fields reconstruct 9,000 years of man's life, tracing domestication of corn and other plant foods. See especially Richard S. MacNeish's summary, pp. 290–309.

Caldwell, Joseph R. "Eastern North America." In Braidwood and Willey, pp. 288–308.

Collier, Donald. "The Central Andes." In Braidwood and Willey, pp. 165–176.

Daniel, Glyn. *The First Civilizations*. Crowell, New York, 1968. A British archaeologist credits the New World with three out of seven of them.

FURTHER READING

Ekholm, Gordon F. "Transpacific Contacts." In Jennings and Norbeck, pp. 489–510. The case for and against such contacts is argued in *Handbook of Middle American Indians*, vol. 4, University of Texas Press, Austin, 1966, by Robert Heine-Geldern, pp. 277–295, and Philip Phillips, pp. 296–315. Illustrations of striking coincidences in art motifs among unrelated cultures are presented by Alfonso Caso in *Cuadernos Americanos*, Mexico City, in vol. 125 (Nov.–Dec. 1962), pp. 160–175, and vol. 143 (Nov.–Dec. 1965), pp. 147–152. The trans-Pacific question is also discussed by Willey, pp. 21–24, and Jennings, pp. 174–176, 333–334.

Elting, Mary, and Michael Folsom. *The Mysterious Grain: Science in Search of the Origin of Corn*. M. Evans, New York, 1967. For young readers.

Haury, Emil W. "The Greater American Southwest." In Braidwood and Willey, pp. 106–131.

Kidder, Alfred, II. "South American High Cultures." In Jennings and Norbeck, pp. 451–486.

MacNeish, Richard S. "The Origins of New World Civilization." *Scientific American* 211:5 (Nov. 1964), pp. 29–37. Discoveries in the Valley of Tehuacán, Mexico.

Mangelsdorf, Paul C., Richard S. MacNeish, and Walton C. Galinat. "Domestication of Corn." In Caldwell, pp. 360–379. (Also in *Science* 143:538–545, Feb. 7, 1964, and 145:659, Aug. 14, 1964.)

Meggers, Betty J. "North and South American Cultural Connections and Convergences." In Jennings and Norbeck, pp. 511–526.

Nordenskiöld, Erland. "The American Indian as an Inventor." *Journal of the Royal Anthropological Institute of Great Britain and Ireland* 59 (1929), pp. 273–309. (Also as Social Sciences Reprint No. A-386, Bobbs-Merrill, Indianapolis, Ind.)

Rouse, Irving. "The Intermediate Area, Amazonia, and the Caribbean Area." In Braidwood and Willey, pp. 34–59.

Wauchope, Robert. "Southern Mesoamerica." In Jennings and Norbeck, pp. 331–386.

West, Robert, ed. *Natural Environment and Early Cultures*, vol. 1 of *Handbook of Middle American Indians*. University of Texas Press, Austin, 1964.

Willey, Gordon R. "Mesoamerica." In Braidwood and Willey, pp. 84–105.

The later opulent culture of the Pacific Northwest is described in Spencer and Jennings, pp. 168–212. Driver, p. 80, gives instances of the planting of wild seeds. For the spread of farming into Europe, see Clark and Piggott, pp. 224–261, and Deetz, pp. 124–125. Macgowan and Hester, pp. 7–9, give examples of Indian inventiveness; Driver, pp. 73–76, lists 181 cultivated plants of native North America and on pp. 554–557 shows the magnitude of the Indians' contribution to the world's food supply. See also Braidwood and Willey, pp. 330–359;

Chard, pp. 183–219; Clark, pp. 70–93, 278–300; Clark and Piggott, pp. 156–181; Driver, pp. 66–83; Jennings, pp. 165–285; Macgowan and Hester, pp. 261–276; Sanders and Marino, pp. 40–50; Spencer and Jennings, pp. 57–99; Willey, pp. 78–245, 267–341.

j970.1 Coy, Harold
C839m   Man comes to America. Illus
by Leslie Morrill. Little,
1973. 150p illus. Bibl.

595

MAR 2 0 1974

INV. 78

NEW HAVEN
FREE PUBLIC LIBRARY